FOLK
LITERATURE
AND CHILDREN

FOLK
LITERATURE
AND CHILDREN

An Annotated Bibliography
of Secondary Materials

Compiled by
George W. B. Shannon

GREENWOOD PRESS
Westport, Connecticut • London, England

Library of Congress Cataloging in Publication Data

Shannon, George.
    Folk literature and children.

    Includes indexes.
    1.   Folklore and children—Abstracts and criticism.
2.   Tales—History and criticism—Abstracts.   3.   Folklore
and children—Bibliography.   4.   Tales—History and
criticism—Bibliography.   I.   Title.
GR43.C4S5   016.3982′088054   81-6432
ISBN 0-313-22808-6 (lib. bdg.)   AACR2

Library of Congress Catalog Card Number: 81-6432
ISBN: 0-313-22808-6

First published in 1981

Greenwood Press
A division of Congressional Information Service, Inc.
88 Post Road West, Westport, Connecticut 06881

Printed in the United States of America

10 9 8 7 6 5 4 3 2 1

To my parents:
For all the tales they shared with me,
And all that's grown from them . . .

CONTENTS

PREFACE

Since the publication of John Locke's *Some Thoughts Concerning Education* in 1693, writers in numerous fields have concerned themselves with the relationship of folk literature and children. It is hoped that this bibliography will afford the educator, librarian, storyteller, and others easier access to the myriad of such materials in English. Journal and magazine articles that have addressed this topic range greatly in style and form. Satirical essays are included, as well as scholarly research and lighter popular articles. Monographs and sections of books included reflect this variety as well. Nonpublished materials are included only in the form of dissertations, theses, and ERIC documents. The bibliography's scope extends from 1693 through 1979. Materials are limited to those concerned with the combination of children and folk literature. Materials dealing only with storytelling techniques or the nonliterary elements of folklore (for example; superstitions) are not included. Though expansive, this bibliography makes no claims to being inclusive. Manual and computer searches were done in all related subject areas, and it is believed that all major writings are included. Older journal articles and those in lesser known sources proved at times impossible to locate. The different library policies regarding the acquisition and loaning of theses and dissertations posed similar difficulties when they had not been reproduced by University Microfilm. Such materials of obvious value are included in the bibliography, but without annotations.

Materials are divided into three categories as determined by their primary topic: Literature, Education, and Psychology. Due to the broad nature of many of the entries, these divisions are at times arbitrary. It is hoped that the subject index will provide full access to these materials. All annotations are noncritical summaries of the materials and are intended to introduce the works to the reader. Entries are organized alphabetically by author within each category. If the author is unknown, materials are listed by title. Entries are coded by consecutive numbers throughout the bibliography. Journal citations include author and joint author, title, journal, volume, date, and pages. Sections of books are cited by author of the selected material, title of book, author or editor of the book, place of publication, publisher, date, and pages. Bibliographic information for ERIC documents includes author, title, ERIC number (for example, ED 123 456), and date if available. Dissertations and theses are cited by author, title, institution of study, and level and date of degree. In instances where an entry is known to have been printed in two sources or reprinted, both sources are given.

Indexes are provided for subjects, authors, and titles. Subject entries include all pertinent words of the title and content, and individuals and specific folk tales discussed in detail. The title and author indexes are self-explanatory. All indexes are coded by the materials' entry numbers.

I would like to thank the two reference departments in Eau Claire, Wisconsin. The McIntyre Library at the University of Wisonsin-Eau Claire provided excellent help, particularly through interlibrary loan without which many of the materials would not have been located. Also of great assistance was the interlibrary loan service of the L. E. Phillips memorial Library/Indianhead Federated Library System. Both proved research can indeed be done in small midwestern cities if one has considerate and skilled librarians. Appreciation is extended to Ray, Nancy, Gary, Sharon, Cleo, and Anne for their kind shoulders during this project, and to Kate Durning and Frada Mozenter for the sparkling philosophical dialogues we shared. And especially to Anne McConnell, dear friend and mentor, I give my warmest thanks, for it was she who suggested Greenwood Press and as always said, "Do it!"

INTRODUCTION

Leaders in the fields of literature, education, and psychology have debated the values and results of sharing folk literature with children since the inventions of printing and of childhood as a social phase. Previous to printing there was little interest in, or manner of controlling, children's exposure to folk tales. Books can be banned or censored; oral conversations and memory cannot. While some tales were designed specifically for children, the majority were not. Children in most preliterate cultures were present at most gatherings and shared in the storytelling and lore of their village or tribe, just as in more modern times children read adult literature such as *Gulliver's Travels* because they found it interesting. Folk tales in these early cultures formed the core of their educational systems, and still do for many (see entries 231, 257, 329, 355). They were entertainment—the early equivalent of television, film, radio, and books combined—but they also passed down the history and mores of the cultures.

Educators were the first to concern themselves with the propriety of telling folk tales to the children of the literate and elite. Progress was the byword, and elements of the past and primitive were to be left behind as civilization moved forward. Literary relics in the form of folk tales became taboo. Though Plato (see entry 348) had long before judged folk tales to be important elements of education, educators considered them to be counter to proper education and harmful to the child's mind. Jean-Jacques Rousseau (see entry 361) was particularly critical of tales for the young child and was a great influence in his time. He saw the modern world as realistic, with no place for frivolity or flights of imagination. Reading, writing, and arithmetic were considered far more important than anything folk literature could offer—if it had anything to offer at all.

Yet, like a cork that cannot be sunk, folk tales continued to thrive and with unrecognized assistance from adults. Literate adults, wanting the best for their children, sent them to schools and hired nursemaids to care for them. These nurses were not elite nor were they always literate, and they continued to follow the natural folk process from which they came (see entry 276). Their parents had told tales to them, and these servants passed them on to the children under their care. There are many children who remember well the tales their nurses told them (see entry 44). In an almost undergound manner folk tales became the property of children within the literate populace. The stories persisted and it was only vainly literate adults who pretended such tales did not exist. Children were eager to acquire literature that offered more interest and adventure than the pabulum being written for them by adults. "Jack and the Beanstalk" captured a child's attention far better than "The Entertaining, Moral and Religious Repository" (1799), for example.

A primary concern regarding the exposure of children to fairy tales is fear. Adults worry that children will be frightened by tales, or moved to violent behavior as a result of being influenced by them. Since Sigmund Freud wrote in 1913 (see entry 426) that "psycho-analysis confirms us in our recognition of how great an influence folk fairy-tales have upon the mental life of our children," those concerned have taken that "influence" as support for their negative viewpoints. Tales are heard during the time in a child's life when basic behavior patterns are established. Some researchers have attempted to show a direct connection between mental illness and hearing tales as a child (see entry 19). Others (see entries 422, 445) acknowledge the connection between tales heard as a child and neurotic behavior, yet view the correlation as a fortunate link and an element to be used in treating the person. This allows the therapist to deal with the adult's problem via his memories and favorite childhood stories.

Far from seeing folk tales as a harmful element, Vaclav Cvrteck (see entry 32) feels they are a "preventive vaccination of children to protect them against dryness of spirit, against lack of emotion, against lower sensitivity to beauty. . . ." Even among those who acknowledge that tales can frighten a child, such as poet W. H. Auden, there is the view that such problems may exist if the tale is heard only once but that familiarity with a tale reduces the fear element, and repetition allows one to master fears and concerns.

The debate is constant. For every writer speaking out for fairy tales there is another who feels they are as terrorizing to children as cruel nursemaids (see entry 459). Just as different opinions exist today regarding the influence of television on criminal behavior, so are there many opinions concerning the influence of folk tales on children. Once again it is the interpretation of Freud's term "influence" which aligns those in controversy. Franz Winkler (see entry 460) finds that "many years of caring for problem children have convinced us of the protection from anxiety and criminal urges that folklore affords." In their impassioned pleas for either point of view, many people forget there are two complex variables involved. Both the tale and the child are different and changing constantly with each interaction. The well-known tale "The Gingerbread Boy" has been condemned as a sick story (see entry 263), applauded as a tale rich in sensory appeal for the youngest child (see entry 204), and dismissed as innocuous by the leader of the realism movement Lucy Sprague Mitchell. Depending on the child and the situation, all these descriptions could be right.

Closely related to the concerns of folk literature and violence is the debate regarding the morals or lack of them in folk tales. Taken literally, Goldilocks steals as does Jack in "Jack and the Beanstalk." Puss in Boots becomes successful by way of deceit (see entry 229). Because folk tales grew out of past times and cultures, some people think they are too primitive for contemporary values. They feel they were created by the masses, and are therefore inferior (see entry 382). How could a story that involves murder, magic, and trickery be of value morally? ask those who oppose fairy tales. Yet those approaching folk literature from a different perspective see great value in sharing tales and rhymes and consider them an element of moral education (see entries 13, 392, 399). G. K. Chesterton found them decidedly moral: "Not only can these fairy-tales be enjoyed because they are moral, but morality can be enjoyed because it puts us in a fairyland, in a world at once of wonder and of war" (see entry 25). A few proponents even extend the folk tale's value to the level of spirituality and see it as a poetic representation of perpetual truths, which, when respected, can serve as a natural guide for children to religion (see entries 312, 460).

A continuing criticism of fairy tales stems from their early condemnation by Rousseau. Folk literature was viewed as frivolous—of the distant and hopefully forgotten past. Lucy Sprague Mitchell (see entry 101) greatly influenced the world of children's literature during the early 1900s with her "here and now" philosophy. Mitchell thought folk tales were out of step with the times (1921) and as a result, harmful to children. How could children learn from tales and rhymes filled with archaic English? It was considered important that tales be educational. Those populated with royalty, talking animals, and magic had nothing to offer the child of the modern world in the eyes of the realists. Robert Dinkel urged parents to find stories instead that were "pertinent to the child's culture, particularly to the commonplace activities of his family and community" (see entry 254). Critics found the language, characters, and events of folk tales of little value so they supplied children with realistic literature instead, such as "The Red Gasoline Pump," a story included in Mitchell's anthology of "here and now" stories. Tales such as "Cinderella" and "Jack and the Beanstalk" were felt to confuse the child and delay his rationalizing of the world. If the meaning of a story could not be seen in one's immediate and tangible life, its usefulness was in grave question. Still, the debate continued in this vein as in all others. Laura Kready (see entry 302), in direct contrast to Maria Montessori (see entry 246), thought folk tales were useful for improving one's study of nature and important to a child's development. Rather than being nonrealistic and fanciful, supporters of the fairy tale believed them to be logical and excellent preparation for the realistic future of adulthood (see entries 27, 141). They felt that children could mature by learning only scientific facts, but feared that without exposure to folk literature they would be sorely lacking in the moral lessons of fairy tales (see entry 212). The polemics persist, with various factions faulting rhymes for being irrelevant and irreverent (see entry 108), while others (see entry 14) praise the same folk literature for its strong characters and events that match the zest and toughness of the contemporary American child.

One school of thought condemns the folk tale for its fanciful qualities, while another offers laurels for its levels of fantasy and imagination. Tales and their telling were and are viewed by many as an aid in developing a child's imagination and creativity, characteristics needed for original work in any field, be it dancing, physics, or teaching (see entry 237). Others support folk literature because of its vicarious elements and the multiple ways it fosters growth of Self (see entries 406, 451). European educator Friedrich Froebel believed children are attracted to such stories by a spiritual life within the tale which shows children themselves (see entry 272). Folk tales are felt by those of this belief to be not of the extraneous past, but rather "treasures of wisdom if we can only develop the capacity to hear that wisdom. Stories allow us to find that wisdom and see that change is possible" (see entry 146).

Among those who favor the sharing of folk tales with children, there are two basic divisions of opinion. One group finds tales acceptable only when they can be used to teach some specific point. They see them as possible elements in lesson plans and of the same value as mimeographed worksheets. They are told or read with a definite objective in mind and children are then evaluated to discern whether or not they "got" the lesson. Here folk literature is not an art, but rather a tool. Those who believe folk tales to be of the arts are always ready to share them, but never with a preconceived purpose in mind other than enjoyment and a shared experience. Adults concerned with all three primary areas addressed in this work—literature, education, and psychology—are divided in this conception of folk literature. Folk tales certainly teach today just as they did in preliterate times, but should they be told only as lessons? Folk tales are literature just as poems are, but should they be dissected and analyzed in an effort to teach literature? Folk tales are certainly bound to the psychological world, but should they be used in a therapeutic manner, and if so, how? Folk art and folk dancing have come to children as easily as tales, but rare are the discussions as to whether or not children should be allowed to dance At Va Ani or view a bark painting from Australia. The worlds of print and education have created a parental sense of protection that constantly oversees the world of folk literatue for children.

Adults control the published world of folk literature for children (adults write, review, and purchase children's books) and there is a perpetual attempt to censor the tales. Personal censorship has been frequent at times, with adults tearing out sections of books or tales and rhymes they did not want their children to read (see entry 156). Even the reasons for censoring the same tale will differ over the years. Tales once censored for violence are now banned for their sexual stereotypes. Tales once widely published are now quietly avoided for their racism. An adult wanting to share a tale with his child from his own childhod will often be surprised. "It's rather disconcerting to pick up one of the old tales to read to your children and then discover that the whole thing's been mutilated in such a disturbing fashion . . ." (see entry 74). This censoring is not done by removing pages, but by rewriting the tales. Comparing editions published in the early part of the twentieth century with the earliest versions is shocking to many. The cute synthetic world of Disneyfied folklore is a recent invention. Censorship under the guise of rewriting is epitomized by cuddly animals, kiss-cures, and a safe blandness that neutralizes the natural strength of folk literature. This form of censorship has created a cluster of Cinderellas and Sleeping Beauties. Depending on the version, Little Red Riding Hood is devoured and the wolf killed, devoured and the wolf freed, or never touched by the wolf at all.

Recently people have begun to criticize and censor folk tales on charges of sexism and racism. The feminist movement called for tales and rhymes with strong female roles (see entries 87, 109, 128). Just as those finding a lack of ethics in tales have charged that folk tales are from the distant past with no relationship to current social behavior, feminists charge the same regarding sex roles (see entry 104). Many propose to discard all such tales, much the same as those who were concerned with violence and immorality did. Again, rewriting the tales also exists. Tales are updated and suddenly Cinderella and Atalanta are cross-cultural. They live in the distant past while exhibiting a 1980s awareness. They no longer marry, but instead open a business. Supporters of the fairy tale such as Alison Lurie (see entries 88, 90) find viable and strong female characters in many of the fairy tales currently in print. Yet depending upon one's sexual politics, the tale "The Fisherman's Wife" is viewed as either sexist or feminist. A balance is struck by those who accept traditional tales as part of the past and as part of all folk literature, including those with a wide variety of sex roles and characteristics. Nancy Ward (see entry 176) urges that materials be added to folk literature rather than tossing them aside or changing them. To rewrite or update traditional tales is "an unforgiveable destruction of our cultural heritage."

Some people question the propriety of "Mother Goose" and claim it exhibits negative self-images and white supremecy (see entry 93). While time has caused some evolution within "Mother Goose," a drastic alteration is not likely to occur, for the modification of folk tales takes decades and centuries. Antisemitic rhymes have gradually been deleted from contemporary editions and so in time, no doubt, will other rhymes that offend a majority of the peoples sharing them. Much folklore tends to be chauvinistic and not all folk literature travels well from culture to culture. "Mother Goose" is as decidedly Anglo-American as "High John the Conqueror" is black-American. While "Mother Goose" is not likely to be banned or successfully rewritten, there has been an increase in publishing additional folk literature from non-Anglo cultures. New editions of tales from black and third world cultures provide expanded exposure for all children. They add to the printed folk literature rather than trying to change what already exists into something beyond its limitations.

Beyond these considerations is the folk literature created by children and shared mostly with other children. While adults have been able at times to control the folk literature they allow for their children, they have no reign on the true folk literature by children, which these children wisely reserve for peers and trusted adults (see entry 120). These tales, rhymes, and songs are filled with a biting and often cruel humor and sexuality. The children's literary paranoia is well-grounded, for most adults who see such folklore will punish a child for his vulgarities—usually the same elements adults enjoy in their own folk humor. In many cases the children's lore even parodies the "proper" folk literature given them by adults (see entry 83).

A tertiary debate exists among those who question whether or not tales are especially for children, not for children at all, or by chance the property of the young. Some, including Tolkien (see entries 142, 164) see no special or innate relationship between tales and children. It happens that many children like folk tales, but tales are not exclusively for them, nor should it be presumed that all children will like them. Those who do not agree with this rather laissez-faire attitude feel there is a direct connection between the folk tale and the child's mind. Just as civilizations passed through oral to written stages of language, so does every child. It is this parallel development that makes the content and process of folk literature excellent material for children (see entry 22). Tales may stem from a less sophisticated past, but they are a fitting correspondence to a child's level of development.

With the number of variables involved—both artistic and human—the crosscurrents of opinion regarding the sharing of folk literature with children will probably continue as long as do the tales and rhymes themselves. As leaders in all fields continue to explore the inner workings of both children and folk literature, new perspectives will, no doubt, be brought to the forefront.

FOLK
LITERATURE
AND CHILDREN

LITERATURE

001. Alvey, Richard Gerald. The Historical Development of
Organized Storytelling to Children in the United States.
Doctoral dissertation, University of Pennsylvania, 1974.

>   Alvey examines the five basic groups concerned with
>   storytelling to children: librarians, educators, reli-
>   gious leaders, recreation specialists and mass media.
>   A general history of such storytelling is discussed in
>   addition to the concern of art for art's sake or story-
>   telling as a pragmatic endeavor. Alvey concludes that
>   when stories are told for any reason besides art it
>   ceases to be storytelling.

002. Applebee, Arthur. "Where Does Cinderella Live?"
The Use of English 25(1973): 136-146.

>   While tales are frequently told to children, it is less
>   certain what the children hear and perceive. Applebee
>   questioned a variety of children about fairy tales and
>   the characters in them and found that children often
>   viewed them in a manner caught in limbo between reality
>   and fantasy. This essay has been reprinted in The Cool
>   Web: The Pattern of Children's Reading edited by Margaret
>   Meek and others. NY: Atheneum, 1978.

003. Arbuthnot, May Hill. "Old Magic: The Folk Tales."
In Time for Fairy Tales: Old and New. rev. ed. Chicago:
Scott Foresman & Co., 1961.

>   Arbuthnot briefly traces the history of the fairy tale
>   and discusses which genres of tales work best with var-
>   ious age groups. Warning against an exclusive diet of
>   fairy tales, she suggests multiple ways of using tales
>   with children.

004. Aries, Philippe. Centuries of Childhood: A Social
History of Family Life. Translated by Robert Baldick.
New York: Vintage, 1962. pp. 95-98.

Aries recounts the place of the fairy tale in 17th
century France and the gradual establishment of these
tales in print for both children and adults. Louis XIII
was himself told fairy tales as a child and his exposure
is seen as typical among the wealthy French of the period.

005.   Arlitt, Ada Hart.   "The Place of Fairy Stories."   In
Psychology of Infancy and Early Childhood.   New York: McGraw-
Hill, 1946.

For its values in verbal development, vicarious experiences and literary references, the fairy tale can not
be omitted from a child's education without ill effects.
The only tales to be avoided are those filled with grotesque images which could easily frighten a child.   All
others clearly add to the "richness of children's experiences."

006.   Armstrong, Helen.   "Hero Tales for Storytelling."
Horn Book 25(1949): 9-14.

Hero tales, with their more complex characterization and
length, are a fine source for sharing with older children.
The length of many hero tales allow them to be told in
cycles of a new installment during each program.   Such
tales provide a form of experience and growth for children much as adults derive from theater.   A bibliography
of hero tales is included.

007.   "The Art of Storytelling."   Littell's Living Age,
17 February 1912, pp. 440-443.

A child who has no books creates his own library of
dreams and tales told to him.   Folk tales and their
remembrance come naturally to children if they are not
taught to read too soon.   Storytelling maintains the
child's natural sensitivity to words and imagination.

008.   Auden, W. H.   "Grimm and Andersen." In   Foreword and
Afterwords.   New York: Random, 1973.

Believing the Grimm tales to be a vital element in a
child's education, Auden takes to task the arguments
that fairy tales are out of date and frivolous.   Broadly
speaking, the fairy tale is a dramatic projection of the
life of the psyche in symbolic images and such can travel
from culture to culture.   "No fairy story ever claimed
to be a description of the external world and no sane
child has ever believed it was."   If a tale is told and
enjoyed then it is viable.   In answer to those who believe tales frighten children, Auden feels that such
fears are mastered when tales are heard several times
and the child becomes familiar with the story.

009. Auden, W. H. "Interlude: the Wish Game." In The Dyer's Hand and Other Essays. New York: Random, 1962.

Auden finds folk tales--which were primarily intended for adults--to have suffered from the idea that tales are either entertainment for children or documents for anthropologists. The evaluation of tales in print is not really possible for they were created for the ear, not the eye. Auden concludes by discussing French and German tales and includes the text of a lesser known variant of "Little Red Riding Hood."

010. Babcock, Mildred D. "What Children Know About Fairy Tales." Elementary English 26(1949): 265-267.

After interviewing all six levels of an elementary school in Illinois, a storytelling class found that children love and know best tales of the past. Among the most popular were "The Three Bears" and "Little Red Riding Hood" and other European folk tales.

011. Baker, Christine H. "The Child's World." Saturday Review of Literature, 5 April 1930, pp. 906.

Rejecting a bookseller's advice that fairy tales were bad for children, Baker bought and read Grimm's tales to a five-year old who thoroughly enjoyed the witches, red hot shoes, et al. Terrible fates do occur in tales but only to the cruel. Baker's child listener found all things justly governed within the tales and was not up-set by any of the events.

012. Becker, May Lamberton. "The Fairy Tale Age and Where It May Lead." In First Adventures in Reading: Introducing Children to Books. New York: Frederick Stokes, 1936.

When a child believes, the fairy tale may take complete possession of him without destroying his sense of the outer world. Becker acknowledges that while a few child-ren will be frightened by tales, the majority love them and some develop a great appetite for them. For many, tales answer their needs and interests in magic. A bibliography is included.

013. Betzner, Jean. Exploring Literature With Children in the Elementary School. New York: Teachers College, Columbia University, 1943. pp. 54-56.

Seeing folk tales as opportunities to see life object-ively, Betzner supports the use of fables, fairy tales and myths with children. Tales represent persisting values, universally accepted beliefs, and their themes appeal to children as well as adults. Even tall tales should be valued for they show what groups of people wish to be like.

014. Bodger, Joan. "Mother Goose: Is the Old Girl Relevant?"
Wilson Library Bulletin 44(1969): 402-408.

Though the language of the inner-city child is far from
classical English, Mother Goose rhymes have much to offer
such children. They aid language development and present strong characters and events worthy of the city
child's zest and toughness. Bodger recommends exposing
children to numerous editions of Mother Goose.

015. Bonner, Mary Graham. "Imaginative Books, Fairy Tales,
Myths." In A Parent's Guide to Children's Reading. New
York: Funk & Wagnalls, 1926.

Bonner discusses the vitality and vital element fairy
tales play in children's lives and imaginations. She
responds to those who question their value and condemns
those who attempt to modernize fairy tales by rewriting
them.

016. Bowen, Elizabeth. "The Comeback of Goldilocks et al."
New York Times Magazine, 26 August 1962, pp. 18-19.

The author welcomes the fairy tales' returned popularity,
for they have much to offer children. Not only are they
aesthetic, but they fulfill the child's interest in
justice. Fostered too by the tales is the child's joy
of discovery.

017. Brady, Margaret Katheryne. Navajo Children's Narratives: Symbolic Forms in a Changing Culture. Doctoral
dissertation, University of Texas at Austin, 1978.

Brady examined the genre of Navajo children's narrative
known as "skin walker" stories. She studied the relationships of the tales with the tellers, purpose of
telling and symbolic resources in the community. Findings demonstrated the way traditional symbols persist
via adaptation.

018. Brooks, Jeanne R. "Do You Have the Phone Number of
the Castle? or Sex Stereotyping in Folk and Fairytales."
North Carolina Libraries 36(1973): 3-6.

Brooks analyzed sex roles in Told Under the Green Um-
brella, a collection of folk tales for children. Of
the twenty-five stories included, only two portrayed
women with good ideas. Most female characters were
peripheral and passive prizes for masculine achievement.
"However no story shows a brave and aggressive girl
getting a handsome man; and no story shows a kind and
good man winning a beautiful girl." Brooks concludes:
"Since trade books seem to be reflecting our changed
ideas about sex roles, we may find our folklore beginning
to change, our mythology being rewritten..."

019. Bruce, H. Addington. "The Fairy Tale and Your Child."
Good Housekeeping, September 1915, pp. 325-331.

Bruce strongly advises against telling children fairy
tales with any violence in them. Relating several cases
of psychotic behavior in adults, he attributes the problems to having heard violent tales as children. Bruce
acknowledges that such children no doubt have a pre-
disposition for impressionability, but asks parents how
they are to know if their child is such until after the
damage is done. At the same time Bruce states nonbrutal
fairy tales provide a rich opportunity for cultivating
the imagination and suggests a general reform of the
fairy tale is "needed for the development and maintenance
of a true civilization." This last comment stems from
his observation that all the presently (1915) warring
countries were bred on fairy tales.

020. Brun, Victor. "Once Upon a Time..." Contemporary
Review 153(1938): 726-733.

The author discusses the history of the Grimm's tales
and their present (1938) acceptance. Seeing the tales'
primary purpose as being to amuse children, Brun feels
the fairy tale does not pretend to educate. The stories,
in his opinion, are beyond the realms of reality and
their horrors are as unreal as their princessess.

021. Callaway, Lynn. "Introduce Your Child to his Family
by Telling Stories of Your Forebears." Parents Magazine,
January 1946, pp. 22-23.

The sharing of family lore can be both an alternative
to printed literature and an exciting tie to one's past.
Callaway feels such storytelling from parents to children establishes an understanding of foreign nations
from whence ancestors came.

022. Capek, Karel. "Towards a Theory of Fairy Tales." In
In Praise of Newspapers and Other Essays on the Margin of
Literature. Translated by M. and R. Weatherall. London:
George Allen and Unwin Ltd., 1951.

Capek closes his general essay on the life and form of
fairy tales with a discussion of why such tales are now
the property of children. He finds fairy tales to be in
the child's world because only small children have re-
mained at the stage before writing was discovered and
because in the young child prehistoric man is preserved
and repeatedly born anew.

023. Cawthorne, Edythe. "Storytelling and Roots."
School Library Journal, April 1977, p. 5.

Cawthorne writes of the importance of storytelling within
the family and discusses the impact the television
film "Roots" has had on people's awareness of family
lore and storytelling.

024.   Chesterton, G. K. "The Dragon's Grandmother." In
Tremendous Trifles. New York: Sheed and Ward, 1955.

The author offers an impassioned plea that the refusal
of fairy tales to children is a major error and would
be done only by those corrupt of heart. Fairy tales are
of common sense and show that the soul is sane. The
Grimm tale "The Dragon's Grandmother" is used as an
example.

025.   Chesterton, G. K. "Fairy Tales." In All Things
Considered. London: Metheun and Co., 1908.

Chesterton discusses the moral aspects of the fairy
tale and that world's strict balance of behavior. "Not
only can these fairy-tales be enjoyed because they are
moral, but morality can be enjoyed because it puts us in
fairyland, in a world at once of wonder and of war."

026.   Clark, Carol. "My Grandmother Told Me a Story About:
Folklore in a Secondary Short Story Unit." Folklore Forum
6(1973): 245-250.

The folk tale is both an effective and enjoyable introduction to the study of the short story. Its scope
offers endless material for background on the American
short story, for so much of the finest literature utilizes
folk literature.

027.   Coggins, Herbert L. "More Red Blood in Mother Goose."
North American Review 233(1932): 464-470.

Discussing various examples, Coggins criticizes those
who censor nursery lore in attempts to protect children.
Nursery lore as it exists prepares children for the
realistic future.

028.   Colum, Padraic. "The Storyteller's Story: the Power
of Imagination." New York Public Library Bulletin 70(1966):
528-532.

Colum relates his childhood in Ireland and the rich
effects of his constant exposure to folk literature
shared in the oral tradition.

029.   Crabbe, Katharyn F. "Folk Over Fakelore: But Is It
Art?" School Library Journal, November 1979, pp. 42-43.

The author examines the transition of folk tales from
oral tradition to print. Because of the differences in
media, strict printings of tales for children may be the

most technically authentic, but they may be lacking the
artistic sense of story and life. The story is more
important than the surrounding details: "documentation
and annotation must be unobtrusive, and...contextual
information is best integrated into the plot."

030. Crabbe, Katharyn F. "Folktales for Children: Literature or Lore?" ED 165 176. 1978.

Crabbe discusses the differences between folklore and
fakelore while showing by examples the problems in retelling or translating tales for children. Rewritings
must be done without damage to the tale's culture, but
need not be bound to footnotes. Tales should "bring
children to love and delight in a culture as well as
to know it."

031. Crossley, Winnifred Moffett. "Storytelling and the
Flowering of the Spirit: the Spiritual Aspects of Storytelling." Illinois Libraries 44(1962): 662-667.

Crossley discusses the riches of tales and telling as
ways of opening up the spiritual world of children.
Tales allow children freedom and awareness, self-
discovery and imagination. "The crystal smallness and
wholeness of a tellable tale make for a relatively quick,
intense experience which children understand and which
they enjoy...." Folk tales offer themes with intrigue
and unobtrusively instruct children.

032. Cvrteck, Vaclav. "Speech." In Give Children the Best:
International Conference of Writers and Theoreticians of
Literature for Children and Young People. Dobris, Czech-
oslavakia. 1975.

Seeing the fairy tale and the child as synonymous and
inseparable, the author in this brief essay views tales as
a "preventive vaccination of children to protect them
against dryness of spirit, against lack of emotion,
against lower sensitivity to beauty..."

033. Dalgliesh, Alice. "An Introduction to the Fanciful."
In First Experiences With Literature. New York: Scribners,
1932.

Children of age four and older should certainly experience fairy tales and a world of fantasy, yet this is
best done by gradual introduction. Many tales are simply
too frightening for children, and it is best to begin with
tales such as "The Three Little Pigs" and "The Three
Bears." Dalgliesh closes by stating that at all ages a
"wholesome balance should be kept between fact and
fancy."

034. Dalgliesh, Alice. "When To Tell Stories To Children."
In Storytelling, edited by Association for Childhood Education. Washington: Association for Childhood Education, 1942.

> Dalgliesh feels the best times of sharing tales are any
> times that suit. An individual with tales ready to
> share can manage most situations by easily sharing him-
> self and a story. The child remembers the tale told
> unexpectedly and naturally more than those shared at a
> regularly appointed time and place.

035. Davis, Robbie L. A Critical Study of Nursery Rhyme
Interests of First and Second Grade Pupils in the Elementary
Department of the Booker T. Washington High School, Mont-
gomery, Alabama, 1951-52. Master's thesis, Alabama State
College for Negroes, 1953.

> Davis read a series of Mother Goose rhymes to first and
> second graders to learn which were more popular and if
> magical or realistic content was a factor in their pref-
> erence. The author's findings indicate that there is
> little difference by grade level of rhymes preferred,
> but shorter rhymes with more simple wording had the
> greatest appeal. Davis encourages the use of rhymes
> with children but "feels those that present "primitive
> cruelty," such as "Three Blind Mice," should be eliminated.

036. Degh, Linda. "Grimm's Household Tales and Its Place
In the Household: the Social Relevance of a Controversial
Classic." Western Folklore 38(1979): 83-103.

> Degh examines the collection of tales gathered by the
> Brothers Grimm and discusses the history of its rela-
> tionship to children. When originally published, the
> book was intended for scholars and included a note of
> caution to adults regarding the sharing of the tales
> with children. Yet, they became very popular with
> children. Hitler demanded that every home own a copy
> and schools were to use it as a textbook. Such educa-
> tors explained "Little Red Riding Hood" with Red
> Riding as the poor folk, the wolf as the Jews and the
> hero hunter as Hitler. While the tales' popularity
> plummeted after World War II, they have gradually come
> into great use again. Degh briefly discusses the
> opposing viewpoints concerning tales and children. The
> tales are completely ingrained in our culture from
> television to film. Though she feels it rarely occurs,
> "Common sense would dictate, as the Grimms suggested,
> that parents, teachers, and publishers make selections
> for the different age groups" rather than giving
> blanket approval or condemnation to all tales.

037.   De Huff, Elizabeth Willis.   "Telling Stories to Primitives."   Bookman 62(1926):   689-691.

De Huff relates her experiences telling European tales to American Indian children and notes their keen sense of lingual rhythm.   These children also have a richer sense of story for the adults around them are still active traditional storytellers.   Only tales of romance failed to interest the children.   Romantic tales embarrassed them.

038.   de la Mare, Walter.   "Introduction."   In Animal Stories. New York: Scribners, 1939.

De la Mare explores the history of folk tales and their multiple thematic relationships to people of all ages. The author closes his essay by discussing the tales' most personal meanings and bond to young children.

039.   Dickens, Charles.   "Frauds on the Fairies."   In Suitable for Children, edited by Nicholas Tucker.   n.p. University of California Press, 1976.

First published in Household Words (No. 184, October 1853), this essay supports the existence of the fairy tale and criticizes the rewritten edition of "Cinderella" and other tales by George Cruikshank.   To emphasize his opinion, Dickens closes with an edition of "Cinderella" as if rewritten by a gentlemen with a great mission.

040.   Donlan, Dan.   "The Negative Image of Women in Children's Literature."   Elementary English 49(1972):   604-611.

Donlan examines the standard rhymes and tales for children and finds them filled with stereotypic images of women.   Females are portrayed as being either helpless or witch-like, needing to be destroyed.   Females are given most of the negative traits including greed, vanity, and cruelty.   If a woman is aggressive in a fairy tale, she is characterized as a nag.   Today "when women are seeking liberation and equality, a young child's image of what is read to him may be in sharp contrast to what he sees."

041.   Dundes, Alan.   "Folklore as a Mirror of Culture." Elementary English 46(1969):   471-482.

Dundes explores the various genres of folklore and the values of studying them.   He carefully separates children's own folk literature from folklore adults assign to them.   The author encourages the greater use of children's own lore and literature.   Symbolism is also discussed in relation to folk literature and its covert and beneficial powers.

042.   Eaton, Anne T.   "Children and the Literature of Imagination."   In Something Shared: Children and Books, edited by Phyllis Fenner.   New York: John Day, 1959.

Even though an individual may remember few of the tales he heard as a child, the exposure to them was and is important and leaves a rich residue.   As imaginative literature, folk tales spark the listener's imagination and provide a sense of what has gone before him.   This essay was first printed in The New York Times Book Review, 21 June 1942.

043.   Edmonds, Edith.   "Storytelling in the Elementary School Library."   Illinois Libraries 29(1947): 83-85.

Edmonds offers guidance for those wishing to share tales with children and feels storytelling can bring about a deep sense of appreciation for good literature.   As children's spans of interest vary, stories chosen for sharing must consider their age and interest level. The teller must avoid becoming didactic to the point of preaching, for it will negate the tale's relationship to the child.

044.   Ekrem, Selma.   "What Fairy Tales Meant to a Turkish Child."   Horn Book 17(1941): 122-126.

The author recalls her childhood in Turkey at a time when there were no children's books.   Still, her world was filled with the richness of fairy tales as told to her by her nurse. This essay has been reprinted in A Horn Book Sampler: On Children's Books and Reading, edited by Norma R. Fryatt.   Boston: The Horn Book, 1959.

045.   Engler, M. C.   "Message Versus Machine: The Art of the Storyteller."   Catholic Library World 44(1973): 471-477.

Engler views storytelling as an art and feels the sharing of folk literature to be one of the ways of battling the world of the machine.   Outstanding storytellers and their philosophies are discussed.

046.   Escalante, Hildamas.   "Storytelling Around the World: a Symposium, Part V: South America."   Library Journal 65(1940): 624-627.

While storytelling is not frequently done in libraries or schools there, South America has a rich heritage of sharing folk tales with children on an every day basis.

047.   "Fairy Tales in Public Libraries."   Public Libraries 11(1906): 175-178.

At a time when books published for children were sweet and sterile, the folk tale became the adopted literature of children for they offered a "naturalness which these books especially for children lack: the moral is not too strongly urged." The author also urges the condemnation of many literary and contemporary fairy tales as being burlesque.

048. Fay, Lucy E., and Eaton, Anne T. "Fairy Tales." In Instruction in the Use of Books and Libraries. 3d rev. ed. Boston: Faxon, 1928.

Though frequently denounced, fairy tales are persistent and continue to provide children with a wide array of experiences. Tales cultivate the imagination, develop a sense of humor, teach without didacticism and also counteract the rushed tendencies of contemporary life. While urging wise selection of tales for children, the authors reject those who rewrite fairy tales and as a result destroy their strengths and dramatic qualities. A bibliography of recommended tales in included.

049. "A Few Words on Fairy Tales." Putnam's Monthly Magazine, July 1857, pp. 58-62.

The author runs the gamut of memories from folk and fairy tales, witches, spirits, monsters and fairies from around the world. Such tales are viewed as desirable with their "usually generous and manly spirit." Tales stir a child's best sympathies and set his imagination to work. If they pause to think, most adults cannot but look back to memories of fairy tales with gratitude and affection.

050. Filstrup, Jane Merrill. "The Enchanted Cradle: Early Storytelling in Boston." Horn Book 52(1976): 601-610.

In turn-of-the-century Boston folk literature and storytelling became a welcome and major element in the education of immigrants and first generation children. The Boston library actively worked to provide quality oral literature as a contrast to shallow movies and dime novels.

051. Frank, Josette. "Fairy Tales and Fantasy." In What Books For Children? rev. ed. New York: Doubleday, Doran and Co., 1941.

While fairy tales belong in every child's life, it is important that parents know how tales are serving their particular child: whether it be escape from reality or wholesome fantasy. Adults must be careful not to gauge their children's fears by their own adult misgivings, for children frequently enjoy the severe justice of tales and suffer no emotional damage.

052.   Gag, Wanda.   "I Like Fairy Tales."   Horn Book
15(1939): 75-80.

Gag discusses the values and safety of fairy tales
(especially the Grimm tales) and finds no cause for
alarm on any level.   Even when people have tried, there
is no way to keep fairy tales from children.   The tales
are too substantial and too rich to be forgotten.   This
essay has been reprinted in Something Shared: Children
and Books, edited by Phyllis Fenner. New York: John
Day, 1959.

053.   Gates, Doris.   "Six Impossible Things."   Education
Digest, March 1949, pp. 27-28.

The author supports the sharing of tales with children
for their beauty, fun and the way they foster a child's
spiritual values.   In response to those who find tales
too fantastic, Gates cites present-day miracles such as
rockets, electric eyes and X-rays as being even more
fantastic than fairy tale events.

054.   Gesell, Arnold, and Gesell, Beatrice Chandler.
"Literature." In The Normal Child and Primary Education.
Boston: Ginn and Co., 1912.

In their efforts to get teachers involved with fine
literature, the authors discuss the quality of Mother
Goose and the many reasons for sharing the rhymes with
children.   The rhymes cannot be bettered.   They are
imaginative and deal with the unexpected, the unusual,
the grotesque and the deliciously human.   "The whole
story is grasped by the children in its completeness,
yet these small units contain the essentials of more
complex stories."

055.   Glover, T. R.   "The Fairy Tale." In The Challenge of
the Greek and Other Essays.   Cambridge: Cambridge University Press, 1942.

Dealing with fairy tales both as literature and as
instructors of values, Glover discusses the deep and
multiple roots of folk heritage.   With horror he notes
that as late as 1929 Columbia University was still
banning fairy tales from children.

056.   Grider, Sylvia Ann.   The Supernatural Narratives of
Children.   Doctoral dissertation, Indiana University, 1976.

Grider collected children's folk literature of a supernatural nature and examines these tales in regard to
local community, students' backgrounds and the community
and its past.

057.   Grout, Dorothy.   "Telling Hero Tales in the Schools."
Top of the News, March 1958, pp. 52-53.

When working with upper elementary children, the author
shared "The Story of Roland" with great success.   The
long lasting effects of the experience were reported
over the years by her students as they matured.

058.   Gruenberg, Sidonie Matsner.   "Books and Reading." In
Your Child Today and Tomorrow: Some Practical Counsel for
Parents. 3d ed.   Philadelphia: Lippincott, 1928.

The author strikes a balance between those who would
give a child any fairy tale and those who view tales as
unworthy.   The fact that tales exist in every culture
gives reason to believe they have educational and emotional values.   "False as they may be as pictures of
life, they are very helpful teachers of human nature."
A combination of fairy tales and realistic stories is
recommended as best.

059.   Hadas, Elizabeth.   "The Case for Fairy Tales."   In
The Children's Bookshelf: A Parent's Guide to Good Books
for Boys and Girls, prepared by the Child Study Association
of America.   New York: Bantam, 1962.

Whether adults ban fairy tales for excuses of violence
or nonrealism, children continue to find, read and enjoy them as they have always done.   While it is important to protect young children from fears they are not
yet able to handle, censoring tales should not be done.
Tales shared must be selected for the child in mind.
Fairy tales will long be popular for they provide vicarious experiences and allow the child to see himself as
he would like to be.   "Through fairy tales, the child
can explore the vast inner world of imagination, touch
basic springs of feeling."

060.   Hadas, Elizabeth.   "Why Fairy Tales?"   Child Study
Journal 35(1958): 34-36.

Though some children may be frightened by fairy tales
the majority find them fascinating because they are
real rather than realistic.   Children enjoy tales as a
means of exploring other worlds and seeing themselves
as they would like to be.

061.   Halpert, Herbert.   "Folktales in Children's Books:
Some Notes and Reviews." Midwest Folklore 2(1952): 59-71.

Halpert discusses the need for authenticity and scholar-
ship in folk tale collections for children.   Used as
examples are editions by Harold Courlander and Richard
Chase.

062. Hartman, Juliet. "Fairy Tales: Their Trial and Triumph." Hygeia, January 1933, pp. 56-59.

Hartman relates the conflicting viewpoints concerning fairy tales by quoting various leaders in childhood education. Those quoted include Agnes Repplier, Maria Montessori and Lucy Sprague Mitchell.

063. Hawkins, Roberta. "Nursery Rhymes: Mirrors of a Culture." Elementary English 48(1971): 617-621.

By examining children's folk rhymes one may discover much about the culture involved. Foods, dress, mores, etc, are all reflected in a culture's rhymes for children.

064. Hayes, Donald, and others. "The Effect of Rhyme on Preschool Children's Retention of Thematic Information." ED 160 253. 1978.

This study found that while preschool children preferred stories in nursery rhyme form, prose passages evoked a higher degree of recognition of story events.

065. Hazard, Paul. "Fairy Tales and Their Meaning" In Books Children and Men. Boston: The Horn Book, 1944.

Hazard sees fairy tales as being reflecting pools of water--deep and crystal clear. Each child repeats through these tales the "history of our species and takes up anew the journey of our spirit from its beginnings." Children keep such tales alive because they need them.

066. Hazard, Paul. "The Nursery Rhymes of England." In Books Children and Men. Boston: The Horn Book, 1944.

The author gladly finds England filled with rhymes that "spring from the hidden depths of the nation's soul!" While the rhymes may be only vowels and simple cadences, they provide the child a sense of conforming to the general pattern of the world.

067. Herman, Gertrude. "Africana: Folklore Collection for Children." School Library Journal, May 1972, pp. 35-39.

As Americans become more aware of the many African cultures, a growing number of collections of African tales have been published for children. Herman discusses authenticity, translations and problems specific to editions for children. A bibliography is included.

068. Herman, Gertrude. "Folktales for Children." Drexel Library Quarterly, October 1976, pp. 42-53.

Herman discusses basic assumptions about folk literature
and children in regard to behavior and as to whether or
not tales reflect everyday life or literal events. By
utilizing a good folklore collection, the adult can
provide the child with a range of "meaningful reading
and listening experiences."

069.   Hinman, Dorothy. "Understanding Through Folklore."
Phi Delta Kappan 35(1954): 324-326.

The author examines various theories behind folk literature and feels "in its undertones and its instrinsic
significance is so deep and meaningful that it challenges
the scholar to life-long effort, yet on the surface it
is so simple and fascinating that it holds even the
most reluctant child reader."

070.   Hornyansky, Michael. "The Truth of Fables." In Only
Connect: Readings on Children's Literature, edited by
Sheila Egoff and others.   New York: Oxford University Press,
1969.

The author views folk tales as good moral propaganda
and discusses "Snow White," "Hansel and Gretal,"
"Jack and the Beanstalk," and "Rumpelstiltzkin" in that
light. Even when surrounded by cartoons and modern
stories, children remain fascinated with the folk tale
and ask for tales time and again. This is so because
such stories reflect the child's picture of himself and
his family. The child is a dwarf in a world of giants
and witches--the youngest son who finally triumphs.
Hornyansky challenges those who tamper with tales in
attempts to protect young minds. Tales are from the
half-conscious wisdom of the race and "I myself should
prefer to take them, unaltered, as a guide to bringing
up children sensibly: as examples of What Every Child
Should Know, and as lessons presented in so cunning a
fashion that a child can accept them before he fully
understands." This essay was first printed in The
Tamarack Review Autumn 1965.

071.   Horovitz, Carolyn. "The Magic Ring--Telling and
Listening."   Utah Libraries 11(1968): 34-46.

Horovitz responds to Ashley Montagu's call for re-
humanizing society and offering education rather than
instruction by suggesting greater use of storytelling
and folk literature. Tales involve the child and carry
him to new and varied worlds. Familiarity with tales
also gives a fundamental grasp of literary form, plot,
style, etc.

072.   Horrell, Ruth C.   "Fairy Tales and Their Effect Upon
Children."   Illinois Libraries 38(1956): 235-239 and 278-282.

In this two-part article Horrell discusses the definition
of the fairy tale and the various opinions regarding
their sharing with children. The author concludes that
fairy tales have a definite place in literature for
children and that only the unthinking adult would use
tales in a frightening manner.

073. Huck, Charlotte. "Traditional Literature." In
Children's Literature in the Elementary School. 3d. ed.
New York: Holt, Rinehart and Winston, 1976.

Huck opens her chapter on folk literature with an over-
view of the value of such tales for children. Folk
literature is seen as a rightful part of a child's
literary heritage and much more than pure entertainment.

074. Hutchison, Earl R. "These Modern Children's Tales."
Elementary English 35(1958): 456-458.

The author discusses the rewriting of traditional tales
for children that leave the stories limp. "It's rather
disconcerting to pick up one of the old tales to read
to your children and then discover that the whole thing's
been mutilated in such a disturbing fashion--the deli-
cious thrills and anticipations of childhood deleted
apparently without discrimination." "Little Red Riding
Hood" and "The Three Little Pigs" are used as prime
examples.

075. "In Praise of Nursery Lore." Unpartisan Review
6(1916): 338-347.

Alarmed by meeting children who were deprived of fairy
tales and bedtime stories in favor of "modern books,"
the author speaks out for the values of folk literature.
Fairy tales offer the child a great deal and appeal to
his human desire to grow up. Those who prevent their
children from knowing Mother Goose and Grimm can hardly
expect their children to love Homer or Shakespeare for
one feeds into the other. The author believes children
prefer fairy tales to useful books just as they prefer
flowers over vegetables.

076. Jablow, Alta, and Withers, Carl. "Social Sense and
Verbal Nonsense in Urban Children's Folklore." New York
Folklore Quarterly 21(1965): 243-257.

The authors found an increase in folk parodies, chain
tales and obscene lore from a study done twenty years
earlier. The stress now (1965) is on an elaboration of
verbal nonsense. Numerous examples are given in all
genres.

077. Jacob, Helen. "Mirror Mirror on the Wall." Illinois
Libraries 48(1966): 724-726.

Jacob interviewed a number of grade school children
about their feelings regarding folk and fairy tales.
Responses were varied, yet all sensed a point of "out
growing" such tales as one matures. The author questions this situation, believing that tales mirror ourselves and it is perhaps adults most of all who do not
like what the tales have to show them.

078.   Kamenetsky, Christa.   "Folklore Revival in Slovenia:
a Quest for Cultural Identity."   School Library Journal,
May 1974, pp. 23-27.

Always striving to maintain their heritage the Sloven-
ians emphasize the passing on of their folk literature
to children.   The best Slovenian writers contribute time
and talent to children's literature and retellings of
local folk tales.

079.   Keach, Everett T. Jr.   "Occupational Folklore."
Elementary English 36(1959): 575-576.

Keach feels the area of folklore best described as
occupational lore has been overlooked and can greatly
contribute to a school's curriculum.   Just as folk
literature of a geographical culture makes one more
aware of that culture, so works the lore of a particular
group of workers.   Occupational lore is also a fine way
for students to chart changes in that profession over
the years.   Through occupational folk literature and
lore students may experience the fears, hopes, problems
and satisfactions of a variety of working situations.

080.   Kidd, Dudley.   "Surprise Stories." In Savage Childhood: a Study of Kafir Children. 1906. Reprint. New York:
Negro University Press, 1969.

Kidd briefly discusses nursery tales and their sharing
with young children of Gazaland before giving texts of
several tales.   A later page (277) describes the telling
of stories by boys around the fire while the girls coax
an old grandmother into telling them the surprise tales.

081.   Kirk, Russell.   "Children and the Lex Talionis."
National Review 26(1974): 870.

During advisory board meetings for Open Court Publishing
Company the question of bowdlerizing tales was featured.
Bruno Bettleheim stressed the "law of retribution" and
the sound justice system established in folk tales for
children and found no reason for such rewritings.

082.   Knapp, Mary, and Knapp, Herbert.   "Tradition and Change
in American Playground Language."   Journal of American Folklore 86(1973): 131-141

The authors collected and compared a variety of childhood folk terms and relate their different meanings from
around the world. Initial study of American playground
folk literature indicates more homogeneity due to the
mobile population than in other areas and cultures.

083. Krueger, John R. "Parodies in the Folklore of a Third
Grader." Southern Folklore Quarterly 32(1968): 66-68.

Krueger noticed a marked increase in his child's use of
children's folk literature during his third-grade year.
The majority of the rhymes, songs, etc., were parodies
of widely known material. Numerous examples are included.

084. Ladley, Winifred. "Folklore and Legends as Fountains
of Humor." Illinois Libraries 48(1966): 727-732.

Acknowledging that all children may not be fond of the
quiet and elegant tales such as "Sleeping Beauty,"
Ladley discusses the variety and appeal of humorous
folk tales. The sharing of such tales familiarizes
children with different ethnic groups and, as do all tales,
these hold within them essential truths to be shared.
A bibliography is included.

085. Lanham, Betty B., and Shimora, Masao. "Folktales
Commonly Told American and Japanese Children: Ethical Themes
of Omission and Commission." Journal of American Folklore
80(1967): 33-48.

The authors surveyed parents in both Japan and the United
States to learn which tales were most frequently told
to children. These findings were then contrasted by
culture to determine differences in ethical values and
culturation. As most tales were told for entertainment,
ethical themes were found in few tales in either country.
Differences between cultures, however, were found to be
reflected in the tales told.

086. Leacock, Stephen B. "Mother Goose Step for Children."
Forum 79(1928): 365-369.

Leacock, with a serious tongue-in-cheek, discusses the
lack of reason behind censoring and softening tales
for children. Tales such as "Little Red Riding Hood"
and "Jack and the Beanstalk" have no real bloodshed.
Folk tales are simply a way in which children learn of
their world and its harsh realities. This essay has
been reprinted in Horn Book 14(1938): 175-178 and
Something Shared: Children and Books, edited by Phyllis
Fenner. New York: John Day, 1959.

087. Lieberman, Marcia R.   " 'Some Day My Prince Will
Come:' Female Acculturation Through the Fairy Tale."
College English 34(1972): 383-395.

Taking her cue from reviews by Alison Lurie, Lieberman
discusses and dissects Lang's The Blue Fairy Book for
its body of tales depicting weak women who are ruled
by males.   Agreeing that tales of strong women exist,
the author dismisses them from her study as being too
remote and unknown to have had an effect upon girls and
women during their emotional development.   The author
feels that these classical aspects of femininity
are imprinted in children via the tales and reinforced
by their frequent telling.   This essay   has been reprinted in Sharing Literature With Children: A Thematic
Approach, edited by Francelia Butler.   New York: McKay,
1977.

088. Lurie, Alison.   "Fairy Tale Liberation."   New York
Review of Books, 17 December 1970, p. 42.

Lurie dismisses the realistic stories fostered by Lucy
Sprague Mitchell as being in actuality unrealistic.
Fairy tales prepare children for the rigors of adult
life.   This is especially so in regard to feminism, for
fairy tales are filled with strong intelligent females.
Real help or danger is most frequently in the form of an
older woman in the tales.   "To prepare children for
women's liberation... you had better buy at least one
collection of fairy tales."   This essay has been reprinted in Sharing Literature With Children: A Thematic
Approach, edited by Francelia Butler.   New York: McKay,
1977.

089. Lurie, Alison.   "Fairy Tales for a Liberated Age."
Horizon, July 1977, pp. 80-85.

Lurie offers three fairy tales with strong female characters as proof that strong women have always existed
and have always been a part of tales to be shared with
children.   Tales included are "Tomlin," "Molly Whuppie,"
and "Clever Gretchen."

090. Lurie, Alison.   "Witches and Fairies: Fitzgerald to
Updike."   New York Review of Books, 2 December 1971, p. 6.

If one looks beyond the small number of fairy tales best
known and Disney-fied in the United States, one finds
tales filled with all of life including female initia-
tive, courage, resourcefulness and kind hearts.   Such
tales are long remembered by children who are forever
playing the characters out in every day life.   This
essay has been reprinted in Sharing Literature With
Children: A Thematic Approach, edited by Francelia
Butler.   New York: McKay, 1977.

091. MacClintock, Porter Lander. "Folk-Tale and Fairy-Story." In <u>Literature in the Elementary School</u>. Chicago: University of Chicago Press, 1907.

For the seven-year-old child the fairy tale is a natural basis on which to begin his literary education and provides effective contact with imaginative art. Yet, points of caution remain. Teachers must be quite expert before utilizing tales outside the European tradition. MacClintock feels that Grimm, Perrault and Asbjornsen constitute the most authentic tales and are the canon of fairy tales for teachers and children of occidental tradition. One must also guard against too many stories. "For a whole year in which the main stories are taken from the folk-tales, a half-dozen stories will be enough."

092. MacDonald, Margaret Read. <u>An Analysis of Children's Folktale Collections, With an Accompanying Motif-Index of Juvenile Folktale Collections</u>. Doctoral dissertation, Indiana University, 1979.

MacDonald examines the inclusion of "fakelore" into folk collections published for children. Reasons for this inclusion are discussed and a motif index of tales in children's literature collections and 188 picture books is included.

093. McDonald, Mary Palmer. "Rhyme or Reason? A Micro-Scopic View of Nursery Rhymes." <u>Journal of Negro Education</u> 43(1974): 275-283.

The author criticizes Mother Goose rhymes in general as exhibiting concepts of white supremacy and negative self image for all children. Specific rhymes are examined for faulty logic and slanderous remarks. She closes by offering some new rhymes and urges adults to stop reading Mother Goose to children.

094. Mack, Anne. "Function of the Fairy Tale." <u>Dial</u>, 16 May 1914, pp. 411-412.

Mack expresses support for sharing the Grimm tales with children "For the stories must be read in childhood: the definciency cannot be remedied by reading them in maturity. They must grow in our minds with our minds." Mack feels these tales equip children with needed facts about life.

095. MacLeod, Mark. "Through Folklore to Literature." <u>Quadrant</u>, September 1978, pp. 64-67.

Reporting on the 1978 Sidney conference "Through Folklore to Literature," MacLeod discusses various papers given on folklore and children. Emphasized is the

important place and function of story in our lives--
the need to tell and to be told stories. Also stressed
is the vitality of folk literature as shown in The God
Beneath the Sea by Garfield and Blishen as opposed to
the watered down rewrites of so many editions. Children
deserve the richest versions of folk literature as
possible.

096. Mary Joan Patricia, Sister. "Mother Goose to Homer."
Catholic Library World 23(1951): 75-79.

The rich use of language and imagination in nursery
rhymes and tales kindles in the child an openess for
fine literature. Beyond developing the imagination,
folk tales also foster mental, emotional and spiritual
growth.

097. Middleswarth, Victoria. "Folklore Books for Children:
Guidelines for Selection." Top of the News, Summer 1978,
pp. 348-352.

Folklore is a broad subject and Middleswarth believes
materials for children should be prepared with the same
care and authenticity given to adult collections and
editions of tales.

098. Millar, John Hepburn. "On Some Books for Boys and
Girls." In A Peculiar Gift: Nineteenth Century Writings on
Books for Children, edited by Lance Salway. Harmondsworth,
England: Kestrel, 1976.

Millar discusses the various editions of fairy tales
available in 1896. He takes to task Jacobs and especially Baring-Gould for their rewriting and censoring of
tales and applauds Lang for letting the tales in his
collections run their natural course in most cases.
Millar feels that little can be added to "the public
stock of harmless pleasure" presently in print. This
essay was originally printed in Blackwood's Magazine,
March 1896.

099. Miller, George Tasker. "The Kinds of Stories That
Appeal to Boys." In Story-Telling to Live Wire Boys.
New York: Dutton, 1930.

The author feels folk literature is best suited for the
younger child. By the third grade what Miller refers
to as "the normal boy" will prefer cowboy tales and
thrillers rather than folk tales. Folk characters
placed at the bottom of the list of favorite tales about
individuals in the author's survey.

100. Milne, A. A. "Introduction Fairyland." In By Way of
Introduction. London: Methuen and Co. Ltd., 1929.

In his introduction to E. S. Hartland's The Science of Fairy Tales, Milne discusses the inevitability of a child's exposure and acceptance of fairy tales. Fairy land, Milne believes, offers the "most tender of all virtues, Simplicity."

101. Mitchell, Lucy Sprague. "What Language Means to Young Children." In Here and Now Storybook. rev. and enl. ed. New York: Dutton, 1948.

Mitchell's famous introduction and treatise on the "here and now" genre of children's literature had much influence. While viewing such "innocuous" tales as "The Gingerbread Boy" as acceptable in moderation, Mitchell condemns most folk literature as primitive, unrelated to present times and classifies tales along with the circus as confusing the child with empty stimulation. Tales such as "Cinderella" are seen as socially damaging and "Does not 'Jack and the Beanstalk' delay a child's rationalizing of the world and leave him longer than is desirable without the beginnings of scientific standards?" Mitchell offers alternative stories that she feels better suit the needs of children, such as "The Red Gasoline Pump."

102. Moore, Annie. "Shall We Banish the Fairies?" Parents Magazine, August 1931, p. 29.

In her defense of sharing folk literature with children, Moore urges readers to realize that the more violent tales such as "Bluebeard" are only a few of the vast number of tales available for sharing. The selection of tales per child's age and maturity is the vital element rather than the sharing itself. "Children should not be deprived of the many excellent tales because of prejudice against those that are unfit. Each story should be judged on its own merit."

103. Moore, Metta Christina. "When Grandma Was a Girl." Parents Magazine, July 1965, p. 54.

The author praises the sharing of family folklore and family stories between generations as a method of gaining a perspective of time and the past. One must be also aware of the difference between sharing family tales and merely rambling on of days gone by.

104. Moore, Robert. "From Rags to Witches: Stereotypes, Distortions and Anti-Humanism in Fairy Tales." Interracial Books for Children Bulletin 6(1975): 1-3.

Moore takes to task those who view fairy tales as a needed and positive force in a child's literary life. The times have changed greatly since the tales were written and are counter to contemporary feelings. Moore

suggests adults work to provide literature that does
not have "negative stereotypes and role models, subtle
racism and gross distortions of reality."

105. Morgan, Charles. "Creative Imagination." In Reflections
in a Mirror. 2nd series. New York: Macmillan, 1947.

Morgan discusses the fairy tale's place in creative
imagination and also uses the fairy tale itself as
metaphor for the creative process.

106. "Mrs. Trimmer from The Guardian of Education." In
Suitable for Children, edited by Nicholas Tucker. Berkeley:
University of California Press, 1976.

This is a collection of children's book reviews first
printed in 1805 in The Guardian of Education. Mrs.
Trimmer's dislike of the fairy tale is most apparent in
the final review included in this collection which
denounces the tales for their "vulgarities of expression." She finds "Bluebeard" horrific and "Cinderella"
and "Little Red Riding Hood" absurd.

107. Mumford, Lewis. "Fact and Fantasy." In Green Memories:
The Story of Geddes Mumford. 1947. Reprint. Westport, Conn.:
Greenwood Press, 1973.

Mumford recalls his son's vivid imagination and fantasies during childhood that developed during a time when
fairy tales were all but banned and literature for children stressed the "here and now." In retrospect, he
wonders if the denial of fairy tales made his son's
fantasies more devious in form and content.

108. Nadeau, John. "Mother Goose Exposed!" Education
80(1960): 491-492.

Nadeau finds Mother Goose rhymes to be filled with
violence and cruelty to animals and other humans. "All
those concerned with the welfare of the child should be
wary lest Mother Goose exert possible corrupting influence on the young mind. That violence, corruption, in-
dolence, cynicism, pessimism and anti-intellectualism
permeate...(Mother Goose)...cannot be denied even by
its champions."

109. Nadesan, Ardell. "Mother Goose: Sexist?" Elementary
English 51(1974): 375-378.

The author offers findings from her content-analysis
and literary examination of The Real Mother Goose. Her
data shows a marked difference in role and frequency
of men and women in rhymes with women being portrayed
only in traditional stereotypic roles.

110. Naumburg, Elsa. "The Fairy Tale in the Machine Age."
Child Study 8(1931): 178-180.

    The author discusses the various arguments for an
    against fairy tales quoting Mitchell, Buhler, etc.
    Shared also is E. Buhler's scientific analysis which
    concludes that "The fairy tale avoids all complicated
    thinking. Its importance lies in the fact that the
    simple tale is so thoroughly enjoyed by the child."

111. Nesbitt, Elizabeth. "The Art of Storytelling."
Catholic Library World 34(1962): 143-145.

    Nesbitt responds to the suggestion that story hours be
    dropped from library services by examining storytelling
    as an art form. Through storytelling one can give
    children the magic of the spoken word and interpreta-
    tive powers.

112. Nesbitt, Elizabeth. "A Rightful Heritage." In A
Critical History of Children's Literature, edited by
Cornelia Meigs. rev. ed. New York: Macmillan, 1969.

    The author recounts the many battles over the propriety
    of fairy tales and their use with children. As support
    grew for tales in the 19th century, more and more
    collections were published for children including the
    work of Lang and Jacobs.

113. Nesbitt, Elizabeth. "Shortening the Road." Library
Journal, 1 November 1938, pp. 834-835.

    Nesbitt discusses the many riches of folk literature--
    especially in regard to language and reading. Tales
    provide a true education filled with stimulation and
    inspiration.

114. Nesbitt, Elizabeth. "Storytelling in the Creative
Way." Catholic Library World 36(1964): 230-232.

    Folk literature and storytelling have the unique power
    of recreating for children, in this complex era, the
    wonder of ancient times and emotions. "Storytelling
    enables the teller to reveal to the child aspects of
    life which lie beyond his immediate and narrow exper-
    ience..." Folk tales bind the past with the present
    to create a whole for the child.

115. Newbigging, Thomas. "Lessons Taught By Fables." In
Fables and Fabulists: Ancient and Modern. 1895. Reprint.
Freeport, New York: Books for Libraries Press, 1972.

    While countering the attacks on fable by Rousseau, the
    author discusses the variety and importance of fables
    in relation to children for "The lesson which the fable
    inculcates is indelibly stamped on the mind of the child."

116. Nodelman, Perry M. "What Makes a Fairy Tale Good:
the Queer Kindness of 'The Golden Bird'." Children's
Literature in Education 8(1977): 101-108.

Using the Grimm tale "The Golden Bird" as an example,
Nodelman discusses the child's relationship to the folk
tale. Nodelman views fairy tales as very satisfying to
the child for his world is always changing in response
to new strange things and the tales are filled with
new encounters and the pleasures of acceptance.

117. O'Faolin, Sean. "For the Child and the Wise Man."
New York Times Magazine, 27 March 1955, p. 9.

The fairy tale is a wise and kind thing that captures
the sense of innocence, wonder and happiness in all
those open to it. Folk tales clearly connect contemporary peoples with the primal times.

118. Olcott, Frances Jenkins. "Fables, Myths and Fairy
Tales." In The Children's Reading. Boston: Houghton Mifflin,
1912.

Establishing imagination as a vital human process,
Olcott finds folk literature to be a most beneficial
stimulus during childhood. Careful editing, however,
is needed, feels Olcott, for many tales present perverted
ideas of right. Yet, on the other hand, tales should
not become condescending or overtly didactic. A bibliography is included.

119. "Once Upon a Time: a Collection of Young People's
Folklore." North Carolina Folklore 20(1972): 108-114.

Examples of folk tales prepared by fourth graders are
printed alongside the children's original illustrations.
Also included are weather lore and superstitions the
children gathered.

120. Opie, Iona, and Opie, Peter. "Tradition and Trans-
mission." Times Literary Supplement, 14 July 1978, pp. 799-
800.
The folk literature known by children consists both of
rhymes and tales told to them by adults and those told
to them by peers and self created. Tales and jokes
created by children themselves are often bawdier than
those shared with parental consent and may frequently
be parodies of traditional nursery lore. The manner in
which these rhymes and tales are transmitted is also
discussed. Examples of such lore are shared throughout the article.

121. Parker, Patricia. "What Comes After Mother Goose?"
Elementary English 46(1969): 505-510.

Without forethought, English-speaking children are
introduced to some of the finest poetry through the
myriad of nursery rhymes that fill their preschool
days.   With such a base established, Parker discusses
other forms of poetry that may be used to "capitalize"
on the child's early affinity and interest in verse.

122. Partridge, Emelyn, and Partridge, George. "Fables
and Other Purposive Stories." In Storytelling in School
and Home. New York: Sturgis and Walton, 1912.

Fables and other related "teaching tales" are stories
aware of their instructional nature.   These tales are
often a type of short hand, stirring up memories of
other complete tales rather than any response of their
own.

123. Partridge, Emelyn, and Partridge, George. "Epic
Stories." In Storytelling in School and Home. New York:
Sturgis and Walton, 1912.

The epic story is especially suited for the adolescent
child, for such tales deal with the ideals of a race
or culture.   They can be shared as is the Bible--
initially as an adventure tale and then later the
spiritual drama may be shared.   Epics are a great help
to children for they are inspired by the genius of
the race involved.

124. Partridge, Emelyn, and Partridge, George. "Myth."
In Storytelling in School and Home. New York: Sturgis and
Walton, 1912.

The place of myth in storytelling with children is
complex, for these tales deal with so much that is
adult in nature.   Myths can be shared in one of two
ways: (1)retell them as nature stories or (2)share
them as adventure tales.

125. Pellowski, Anne. "Children's Stories Around the
World." Transcription by Sister Barbara A. Kilpatrick.
Catholic Library World 51(1979): 76-78.

Pellowski discusses the various manner of sharing folk
literature in different cultures and the general decline in oral storytelling.   In her travels to foreign
countries the author found the sheer sounds of a story
to be a fine way of introduction whether words are
understood by children or not.   West African and East
European storytelling is described while Pellowski sees
little effort being made to preserve traditional stories
in Arabic, Turkish and Persian languages.   Children in
these areas are very poor in terms of the oral tradition and the continuing use of folk literature.

126.   Pennington, Harriet D.   "The Lost Art of Storytelling."
Parents Magazine, August 1966, pp. 48-49.

In the past, storytelling was the chief way parents
passed traditions on to their children. Though times
have changed, this form of communication and sharing
is as rich and appealing as ever. Pennington suggests
a variety of tales and forms that children enjoy.

127.   Pfaender, Ann McLelland, and Winstedt, Eloise West.
"Storytelling Around the World: a Symposium. Part IV:
Hawaii." Library Journal, July 1940, pp. 574-577.

The situation of two separate school systems divided
by language (English and Pigeon English) created some
problems in the libraies' sharing tales in these
schools. Careful selection was helpful and fairy tales
from around the world were found to be the most popular.

128.   Phelps, Ethel Johnson.   "Introduction." In Tatterhood
and Other Tales. n.p.: The Feminist Press, 1978.

In this introduction to a collection for children of
tales depicting strong females, Phelps discusses the
problems of sexism in tales and how she went about
easing that problem for her collection. As most tales
were created long ago for adults, Phelps feels it
acceptable to tame violent elements when sharing them
with children.

129.   Picard, P. M.   "Stories Through the Ages: the Great
Oral Tradition." In I Could a Tale Unfold: Violence,
Horror and Sensationalism in Stories for Children.   New
York: Humanities Press, 1961.

Picard explores the rich heritage of folk literature
and recounts the age in which adults and children
shared tales on a daily basis. Then, as now, tales
offered children experiences as yet unknown to them.
While time and media have altered the place of oral
tradition, the tales children accept without hesitation
are still those that hold a mixture of "vigorous simplicity, precise detail and wide scope for the imagination."

130.   Pilant, Elizabeth.   "Family Folklore." Elementary
English 30(1953): 148-149.

Family folklore and its themes can provide rich resources for motivating student writing and research.
Family tales have a lively sense of communication and
have been through the polishing process of generations
of tellings. Students, by doing such work, become
closer to their community and give a voice to their
immediate culture's past.

131.   Ponsonby, Marion.   "One of the Moot Problems of
Education and Parents."   Saturday Review of Literature,
26 October 1929, p. 327.

Children see little to fear in fairy tales and concen-
trate on the victory of the virtuous. It is the adult
mind which clouds the issue by worrying about fateful
events in tales from the adult perspective. To prevent
a child from hearing fairy tales and myths would hand-
icap his comprehension of adult literature.

132.   Price, Leota.   "Story Hour in the Library."   Illinois
Libraries 8(1926): 78-79.

Price relates her library's storytelling programs for
children, the goals of which are to provide a pleasant
and profitable time as an aid to children in growing
into fine adults. Children were encouraged to tell the
tales they had heard. The author expressing the richness of folk literature questions "if we could not get
along without Shakespeare better than Mother Goose."

133.   Rausch, Helen Martha.   The Debate Over Fairy Tales.
Doctoral dissertation, Columbia University Teachers
College, 1977.

Rausch examines the decades long conflicting opinions
regarding fairy tales and children. Two primary developments covered are the turn of the century belief that
tales fostered the child's imagination and the affect
of Lucy Sprague Mitchell's Here and Now Storybook.

134.   Repplier, Agnes.   "Battle of the Babies." In Essays
in Miniature. 1892.   Reprint.   New York: Greenwood Press,
1969.

The author relates the battle in print over the pro-
piety of exposing children to fairy tales. The debate
was fairly well split by the Atlantic with New York
and Boston writers trying to protect sensitive American children while the likes of Andrew Lang in England
supported fairy tales. Repplier herself finds the
tales to be the rightful inheritance of children.

135.   Reynolds, J. D.   "Why Story Hours?"   Junior Bookshelf,
October 1937, pp. 17-21.

Reynolds thoroughly attacks the telling of stories in
libraries as a waste of time and money and claims the
average story hour (England 1937) is an insult to
the child's mentality and critical faculties.

136.   Robert, Marthe.   "The Grimm Brothers." In The Child's
Part, edited by Peter Brooks.   Boston: Beacon Books, 1969.

The author discusses the Grimm brothers and their
collecting of tales. Robert views their tales as
graceful and amusing instruments of instruction: "Its
purpose is serious beneath the appearance assumed for
giving amusement."

137. Roemer, Danielle Marie. A Social Interactional
Analysis of Anglo Children's Folklore: Catches and Narra-
tives. Doctoral dissertation, University of Texas at
Austin, 1977.

Roemer examines the folk narratives of children ages
five through eight near Austin, Texas. Considered is
the relationship between the stylized verbal behavior
of children and social rights and duties which adults
expect. The children's developmental acquisition of
the narratives is also described.

138. Roscoe, William Caldwell. "Children's Fairy Tales
and George Cruikshank." In A Peculiar Gift: Nineteenth
Century Writings on Books for Children, edited by Lance
Salway. Harmondsworth, England: Kestrel Books, 1976.

Roscoe laments Cruikshank's rewritten fairy tales and
calls them "sacrilegious alterations." The only
reason for their purchase is the illustrations. This
essay has been reprinted in Poems and Essays by the
Late William Caldwell Roscoe, edited by Richard Holt
Hutton. Chapman and Hall, 1860. It was first published in The Inquirer, 1854.

139. Ross, Eulalie Steinmetz. "Give Tongue to Literature."
Michigan Librarian, October 1957, pp. 23-25.

Ross sees storytelling and folk tales as a compelling
invitation to read for children. Via tales, children
gather revelations of truth, imagination and laughter--
"the stuff that spirits grow on."

140. Ross, Eulalie Steinmetz. "To Tell a Story." Horn
Book 39(1963): 253-258.

Ross shares suggestions for best sharing tales with
children. Comfort and listening skills of the children should be tended to if the sharing is to go well.
A tale works most successfully when it is one the
teller treasures. Sincerity is paramount when sharing
folk literature with children.

141. Ryan, Calvin T. "Taking Folk Literature Seriously."
Elementary English 30(1953): 146-147.

In response to those who feel folk tales should not be
taken seriously, Ryan discusses tales as vital elements
in peoples lives that were initially viewed with respect. Tales have long served a variety of purposes

for the listeners. "Folk tales are logical. They are
cross-sections of life. They are usually more concerned
with the Truth of Meaning than the Truth of Fact."
Children deserve traditional tales. They were not
given an imagination so that it could be ignored, but
rather guided and cultivated.

142. Sale, Roger. "Fairy Tales." In Fairy Tales and After:
From Snow White to E. B. White. Harvard University Press,
1978.

Sale views fairy tales as being no more for children
than being not for them because tales existed long
before the invention/recognition of childhood. While
agreeing tales have much to offer, Sale criticizes
the over analyzation of those not truely familiar with
fairy tales such as Bruno Bettelheim. A slightly
different version of this essay was published in
Hudson Review 30(1977): 372-394.

143. Sayers, Frances Clarke. "From Me to You." In
Summoned by Books. New York: Viking, 1965.

Sayers sees folk literature and storytelling as aiding
reading and of bestowing color and drama to the written
word. Beyond all else, storytelling provides an inti-
macy of language and literature. The power remains of
the voice and words. This essay was originally printed
in Library Journal, 15 September 1956.

144. Sayers, Frances Clarke. "The Storyteller's Art." In
Summoned by Books. New York: Viking, 1965.

By sharing folk literature orally with young people the
adult introduces to the child fine literature. Through
storytelling the child learns to recognize elements of
creative style--"originality, style, structure and form,
characterization, mood and atmosphere, and the beauty
of words." This essay was first published in 1953 by
the Association for Childhood Education International
as a part of their series Adventuring in Literature
With Children. It was originally titled "Enriching
Literature Through Storytelling."

145. Schmitt, Yvette, and Mary Nora, Sister. "What Are
Some Meaningful Experiences With Literature." Elementary
English 41(1964): 500-510.

Storytelling can meet a child's need for attention,
security, belonging, and aesthetic satisfaction. The
child gains as listener and also as teller from story
experiences, and all encounters increase the child's
acquaintance with literature. Various related activities are discussed and a bibliography concludes the
article.

146. Schram, Pininnah. "Where Are Our Storytellers of
Today?" Educational Forum 43(1979): 175-183.

Man is a storytelling creature and his life is and
should be filled with stories of the past. Today's
children in their multi-media world have become distant
from this element. By sharing tales, children will
develop listening abilities, a sense of form, improved
memory; and tales also give them a chance to question.
"There are treasures of wisdom if we can only develop
the capacity to hear that wisdom. Stories allow us to
find that wisdom and see that change is possible."

147. Schwartz, Alvin. "Children, Humor and Folklore:
Part I." Horn Book 53(1977): 280-287.

Schwartz, through examples, discusses the humorous folk
literature of children, which ranges from jokes to
tall tales. This essay has been reprinted in Crosscurrents of Criticism: Horn Book Essays 1968-1977,
edited by Paul Heins. Boston: The Horn Book, 1977.

148. Schwartz, Alvin. "Children, Humor and Folklore:
Part II." Horn Book 53(1977): 471-476.

The concluding half of this article discusses the more
vicious side of folk literature that grows out of
anxiety and hostility. These elements are expressed
in the moron tales, sick jokes and ethnic stories.
This essay has been reprinted in Crosscurrents of
Criticism: Horn Book Essays 1968-1977, edited by Paul
Heins. Boston: The Horn Book, 1977.

149. Slator, Anne. "Folk Tales For All Folks." School
Library Journal, September 1974, p. 4.

Responding to Taylor's article (#161) Slator urges the
use and sharing of folk tales with all ages of young
people. To presume middle school students don't like
folk tales and to not share them is a disservice to the
students. The author asks if such students don't like
folk tales, then who is checking out the more complex
volumes of folk literature from her library.

150. Smith, Lillian. "The Art of the Fairy Tale." In
The Unreluctant Years. Chicago: American Library Association, 1953.

Smith feels fairy tales play the same part in a child's
imaginative and literary development as any other literary art form. The tales stem from a time and people
that created out of a true art impulse and as such traditional versions should be respected. Using "Sleeping
Beauty" and "The Three Billy Goats Gruff" as examples,
Smith discusses the fine language, form and imagery
of fairy tales.

151.   Soriano, Marc.   "From Tales of Warning to Formulettes:
the Oral Tradition in French Children's Literature."
translated by J. B. Frey.   Yale French Studies 43(1969):
24-43.

Soriano notes that most folk literature designed for
children has a sad or violent ending as they were
created to teach.   The goal is to frighten the child
into proper behavior.   The range of French folk literature for children is great, including all varieties
of rhymes and poems.   These shorter pieces, in part
created by children themselves, are designed for
laughter.   The author views this humor as a needed element if the child is to have faith in life.

152.   Spencer, Margaret.   "Stories and Storytelling."   In
Children Using Language: an Approach to English in the
Primary School, edited by Anthony Jones and Jeremy Mulford.
London: Oxford University Press, 1971.

Spencer examines the various forms of storytelling by
children and relates them to their exposure to folk
literature.   The largest number of stories shared with
children are folk and fairy tales and their style is
apparent in the early writing of children in regard to
straightforward narratives and specialized language.
Among their other virtues, folk tales "offer children
the chance to understand the nature of the spectator
activity by giving them certain conventions within
which to contain experience and look at it."

153.   Stanton, Will.   "Rumpelstiltskin, He Said His Name
Was."   Readers Digest, August 1969, pp. 51-53.

Stanton finds the classic fairy tales just as ridicu-
lous as television programs.   After giving an evalua-
tive summary of Rumpelstiltskin, Stanton decides that
neither medium is better than the other, or worse.

154.   Stone, Harry.   "Dickens, Cruikshank and Fairy Tales."
Princeton University Library Chronicle 35(1973-74): 213-247.

Stone recounts the bitter conflict between Dickens and
Cruikshank over Cruikshank's teetotalling retellings
of several fairy tales.   This conflict led Dickens to
write his famous essay "Frauds on the Fairies," and he
continued to support children's rights to folk and
fairy tale literature.

155.   Stone, Kay.   "Things Walt Disney Never Told Us."
Journal of American Folklore 88(1975): 42-50.

The author discusses the many and varied tales populated with strong females that offer children a more
rounded view of sexuality and personalities.   Disney's

influence on "rewriting" tales to the point of cen-
corship has had an effect on the self concepts of
those children who viewed them as opposed to the
present "post-Disney" generation.

156.   Stone, Wilbur Macey.   "Emasculated Juveniles."
American Book Collector 5(1934): 77-80.

Stone discusses the vast censorship against nursery
rhymes and folk tales in the 19th century.   Printed
editions were carefully edited.   Parents also butch-
ered books by removing pages before letting children
see them.   The author closes by expressing hope that
such molestation does not arise in the future.

157.   Storr, Catherine.   "Why Folk Tales and Fairy Stories
Live Forever." In Suitable for Children, edited by Nicholas
Tucker.   Berkeley: University of California Press, 1976.

Storr disagrees with Tolkien and feels fairy tales are
most suited for children.   She believes so for the
tales' settings are more congenial to childhood.   Tales
should be valued for their form, their message, and
their ability to impose a pattern on what mystifies
and frightens the child.   This essay was originally
printed in Where, January 1971.

158.   Stwertka, Eve Maria.   "Preliteracy in a Postliterate
Age."   ED 153 224.   1977.

Stwertka reports on the college-aged poor reader.   Analysis shows that children not exposed to oral literature do not develop as refined as reading and speech
skills as those who are.   The skills of literary imagination grow out of storytelling and shared folk
literature.

159.   Sutton-Smith, Brian.   "Psychology of Children's
Folklore: The Triviality Barrier."   Western Folklore
29(1970): 1-8.

The author defines childlore and discusses the difficulties and need for serious study of children's folk
literature and lore.   At present there seems to be no
universal language of lore among all children.

160.   Taylor, Mark.   "Television is Ruining Our Folktales."
Library Journal, 15 December 1959, pp. 3882-3884.

While tales have always been altered for new media,
television allows for no audience feedback.   Without
regard for folk literature or people's preferences
television is able to distort fairy tales and then
present them as authentic to children.   While children
are fairly discriminating, after a while they allow

themselves to put up with whatever is available be it
good or mediocre. The censorship qualities of folk
literature on television are also discussed.

161. Taylor, Mary Agnes. "The Folk Tale: Literature For
All Ages?" School Library Journal, March 1974, pp. 80-81.

Using Isaac B. Singer's tale "A Fool's Paradise," Taylor
discusses the structure of folk tales and their wide
appeal. Tales work well with young readers, who enjoy
the action and adventure and equally well with adults,
who are able to explore the symbolism and metaphors.
"Folktales...can be read at face value or for implied
meaning." It is those in the middle grades who fall
in the crack. They resist the childish aura attached
to tales and are not yet able to read metaphorically.
"If librarians expect folk literature to reach matur-
ing readers who are between these poles, they are over-
rating the power of the genre to appeal equally to all
ages."

162. Thigpen, Kenneth, Jr. "Adolescent Legends in Brown
County: a Survey." Indiana Folklore 4(1971): 141-215.

Thigpen shares and discusses a large collection of
adolescent folk literature gathered in Nashville,
Tennessee. Such oral tellers and tales form two basic
groups of lore: (1)counter culture tales and (2)the
stereotypic teenager of the past.

163. Thornley, Gwendella. "Storytelling Is Fairy Gold."
Elementary English 45(1968): 67-79.

The author views tales as fairy gold--something that
must be given away before it has any real value. Tales
of all variety offer much to children and are the natural approach to children's books. A bibliography of
suggested stories and age levels is included as well
as suggestions for learning and telling stories.

164. Tolkien, J. R. R. "On Fairy-Stories." In Tree and
Leaf. Boston: Houghton Mifflin, 1964.

Tolkien's essay on faerie and fantasy literature discusses the histories of the genres and the qualities
of various collections and collectors. He views the
close association of child and tale as a domestic
accident of the nursery and feels fairy tales should
not be specially associated with children.

165. Toothaker, Roy E. "Folktales in Picture-Book Format:
a Bibliography." School Library Journal, April 1974,
pp. 26-32.

The author discusses the values of sharing folk literature with children and offers definitions of various
folk genres. The core of the article is a bibliography
of picture-book folk tales recommended for children.

166. Travers, P. L. "Only Connect." In Only Connect:
Readings on Children's Literature, edited by Sheila Egoff
et al. New York: Oxford University Press, 1969.

Travers reflects on her childhood that was rich with
storytelling and tales and myths. Celtic tales as well
as her favorite Grimm tale, "The Juniper Tree," continue to fascinate her. She feels tales should be
shared with children, but not lightly, and states: "I
think it is more and more realized that the fairy tales
are not entertainments for children at all." Those
who alter tales so as not to frighten children are
counter productive. "...it is better not to tell them
at all than to take out all the vital organs and leave
only the skin." This essay originally appeared in
Quarterly Journal of Acquisitions of the Library of
Congress, October 1967.

167. Trease, Geoffrey. "Fancy Free." In Tales Out of
School. 2nd ed. London: Heinemann, 1964.

Trease briefly addresses the printed history and censorship of the fairy tale and its place in children's
lives. Beyond aspects of entertainment, the fairy
tales' virtues match those of all good children's
books: "To stimulate the imagination...or to educate
the emotions."

168. Treavor, John. "And They Lived Happily Ever After."
National Education Association Journal 37(1948): 606-607.

Seeing storytelling as an important part of an upper
elementary program, Treavor discusses the need for and
methods of teaching children the patterns and dynamics
of folk tales and their telling. Frequent exposure to
traditional fairy tales is beneficial.

169. Trotter, Frances. "Storytelling Around the World:
a Symposium. Part III: Canada." Library Journal, 1 June
1940, pp. 484-487.

Trotter reports on the uses of folk literature and
storytelling with children in Canadian libraries. Also
included are children's reactions as to their favorite
folk tales and genres.

170. Tsonev, Plamen. "Speech." In Give Children the Best:
International Conference of Writers and Theoreticians of
Literature for Children and Young People. Dobris, Czecho-
slovakia, 1975.

Tsonev sees the fairy tale as helping children mature and to discover themselves so that growth may occur and decisions of vocations will be satisfying. Tales aid in the shaping of character, mind and even the potential of machines. The author quotes various socialist leaders in his support of the fairy tale and its value.

171.   Tucker, Elizabeth Godfrey. Tradition and Creativity in the Storytelling of Pre-Adolescent Girls. Doctoral dissertation, Indiana University, 1977.

The folk literature of two different Junior Scout troups is examined. One group was from an academic community and the other was not. The different ways in which the girls are raised affects the variety of tales they tell and create and the role they take as women. Self expression was stronger among the academic community while the girls enjoyed linguistic tricks and "nasty" stories more frequently than the other group.

172.   Vallasekova, Maria. "The Child and the Fairy Tale." Educational Media International 4(1974): 27-34.

The author reports on different Czech studies done involving fairy tales and children including one study utilizing television. Examining the most frequent negative ideas about fairy tales, Vallasekova defends tales and concludes they play a large part in the development of a child's speech, fantasy, emotions, intellectual abilities and his personality as a whole.

173.   Van Stockum, Hilda. "Storytelling in the Family." Horn Book 37(1961): 246-251.

As children listen to a story they are themselves creating. Storytelling is one of the few times an adult (the teller) gives full attention to the child and the child is well aware of this. From a pleasure in listening, the child easily grows to desire the same enjoyment of literature in print.

174.   Viguers, Ruth Hill. "Over the Drawbridge and Into the Castle." Horn Book 27(1951): 54-62.

Viguers relates the past times of traveling troubadours and the eagerness with which adults and children awaited their visits. Today, as then, tales shared can develop a child's appreciation for words and in time books. Through tales children are able to absorb the color and atmosphere of foreign lands and people.

175.   Wahl, Frederick. "Tell More Myths and Legends." Recreation, May 1940, pp. 98-99.

Wahl found that children who clamored for Buck Rogers
were also enthralled with ancient tales such as Beo-
wulf and Maui. Legends told are rarely forgotten and
give the child a rich background.

176. Ward, Nancy. "Feminism and Censorship." Language
Arts 53(1976): 536-537.

Ward cautions those who strive for strong females in
literature for children to guard against censorship.
She urges the use of Mother Goose and folk tales and
the inclusion of tales with strong women. To rewrite
or update tales is "an unforgivable destruction of our
cultural heritage. We want balance, not censorship--
not material taken away but material put in."

177. Weber, Blanche. "Storytelling Around the World: a
Symposium. Part II: Europe." Library Journal, 1 May 1940,
pp. 379-381.

Weber discusses the role of folk literature and storytelling with children in both library settings and
those less formal occasions where tales are simply
shared during work and other daily events.

178. Weber, Rosemary. "Folklore and Fantasy--Mix or Match?"
ED 154 424. 1978.

As oral storytelling occurs less and less, modern media
are taking up its place in terms of presenting fantasies and fantastic worlds to children. While the
forms may have changed to film and the likes of Star
Wars, the basics of folklore and fantasy remain the
same.

179. Weekes, Blanche E. "The Child's First Literature."
In Literature and the Child. New York: Silver, Burdett and
Co., 1935.

The author acts as a balancer for the opposing views
regarding children and folk literature. Standard
elements of condemnation and support are discussed and
compared. A bibliography is included.

180. Welty, Eudora. "And They Lived Happily Ever After."
New York Times Book Review, 10 November 1963, p. 3.

Welty sees the fairy tale as the finest of literature.
Tales are like by children because they are "wonderfully
severe and uncondescending." Fairy tales are pitiless
and filled with intrigue as well as irony, elements
children appreciate. The residue of fairy tales heard
in childhood lasts a life time and enriches all sub-
sequent experiences.

181. Whiteman, Edna. "Storytelling as a Method of Directing the Reading of Children." Playground, April 1930,
pp. 25-27.

> Whiteman discusses storytelling, folk tales and ways
> of choosing the best genre of tale for different age
> groups. She feels, as does H. Mabie whom she quotes,
> that the fairy tale belongs to the child and should
> always be within his reach. "No philosophy is deeper
> than that which underlies these stories; no psychology
> is more important than that which finds its choisest
> illustrations in them."

182. Wilhelm, Robert Bela. "Storytelling is Self-discovery."
New Catholic World, July 1972, pp. 167-169.

> Without sharing in stories one can live only in the
> present and has no sense of past or hope of a future.
> The child is a natural storyteller, for he allows his
> imagination to turn everyday events into adventures
> and series of events into a unified story. Story-
> telling allows one to explore "what can be" rather
> than "what is."

183. Willard, Nancy. "Well-Tempered Falsehood: the Act
of Storytelling." Massachusetts Review 19(1978): 365-378.

> The author describes and discusses her childhood affin-
> ity for storytelling and the Grimm tales. As a writer
> and teacher of writing, she finds the use of oral story
> and folk literature a vital element in her work.

184. Williamson, Terri. "Children's 'Scary' Stories."
Southwest Folklore 1(1977): 44-50.

> Williamson examines over one hundred children's 'scary'
> stories from a variety of sources. Most of these tales
> are learned by children by way of books, film, friends,
> or siblings. Variants of several tales are included.

185. Winslow, David J. "Children's Picture Books and the
Popularization of Folklore." Keystone Folklore Quarterly
14(1969): 142-157.

> Winslow discusses the problems of authenticity in illus-
> trated editions of single folk tales published for
> children. If done well, such books are a definite
> source or manner of presenting and passing on folk
> lore materials to the next generation.

186. Winslow, David J. "An Introduction to Oral Tradition
Among Children." Keystone Folklore Quarterly 11(1966):
43-58 and 89-98.

In this two-part article Winslow discusses the world
of children's folk literature and methods of collecting
it. Both television and print have affected the variants and manner of preservation of children's folk
literature. Winslow feels children are natural storytellers and bearers of the oral tradition because they
cannot write.

187. Withers, Carl. "Current Events in New York Children's
Folklore." New York Folklore Quarterly 3(1947): 213-222.

Wither's collection of children's lore shows a wide
variety of literature that changes most drastically
during times of national crisis as during World War
II. Examples of such tales and rhymes are included
throughout the article.

188. Wolkstein, Diane. "An Interview With Harold
Courlander." School Library Journal, May 1974, pp. 19-22.

Wolkstein and Courlander discuss the process of collecting and adapting folk literature for children. The
problems of cruelty and violence in many tales are
explored as are matters of selection and censorship.

189. Wollner, Mary H. B. "Back to the Classics." Today's
Health, September 1957, p. 20.

Feeling those adults who insist on altering and softening tales for children are themselves immature,
Wollner discusses the child's need and affinity for
folk literature. The ignorance of traditional literature and its heroes may easily lead the child's taste
toward more shallow contemporary heroes as found in
comic books. Through traditional literature the child
identifies with the heroes and "through this identification he may be enabled to acquire a sense of
human destiny."

190. Wright, May M. "Terrible Tales for Tots." Elementary English Review 18(1941): 191-192.

Wright cites a study by the American Library Association which reported that children were indifferent to
fairy tales. She finds this not surprising and feels
the high level of gloom and misery in tales to be a
likely cause. Fairy tales and nursery rhymes are filled
with death and suffering and the language is equally
harsh. "Fortunately, our modern libraries contain a
wealth of non-fiction presented in the vocabulary of
the up-to-date child and youth."

191. Yolen, Jane. "The Fault of the Nightingale: Effects
of Fairy Tales on Children." California Media and Library
Educators Association Journal, Fall 1977, pp. 8-12.

Yolen speaks to the cycle of support and condemnation
of fairy tales and shares her own feelings that fairy
tales give children a greater sense of the world than
"realistic" stories. Folk tales affect and are affected
by those who hear them, tell them and rewrite then for
print. Three versions of "Snow White" (Disney, Hyman
and Burkert) are discussed in regard to interpretation.
While each edition is different, they may all be able
to touch innerselves to help children and others find
their own centers as all stories do.

192. Yolen, Jane. "Mining the Folk Lode." In Writing
Books for Children. Boston: The Writer Inc., 1973.

As an author of children's books, Yolen discusses the
riches of folk literature as a writing genre. Various
forms of tales are examined as well as structural
elements and the considerations to acknowledge when
"retelling" a folk tale on paper.

193. Yolen, Jane. "On Limiting the Folk." School Library
Journal, May 1974, p. 3.

Yolen responds to Taylor's article "The Folk Tale:
Literature For All Ages" (#161) and argues that folk
tales are very well suited to middle school children.

194. Yolen, Jane. "Shape Shifters: Every Child's Adventures in Fairy Tales." Language Arts 55(1978): 699-703.

The child who knows himself to be a dual creature--good
and bad--is especially drawn to folk tales of transformation. Without tales to show us the magical side of
ourselves, we can only be half existent--never whole.

EDUCATION

195. Adler, Felix. "The Use of Fables." In The Moral Instruction of Children. New York: Appleton and Co., 1892.

The author sees the fable as like a flash photograph that fixes one's entire attention on one element. They offer much for children, but must be carefully selected. Adler finds many fables unusable because they are too close to their Asiatic origins and have a spirit of fear and pessimism. Included is a list of fables suitable for children by Adler's standards.

196. Adler, Felix. "The Use of Fairy Tales." In The Moral Instruction of Children. New York: Appleton and Co., 1892.

Adler finds fairy tales of value for they stimulate the imagination, reflect the communion of human and universal life as well as quickening mood sentiments and encourage ideals. Using the Grimm marchen as examples, the author encourages the telling of tales rather than the reading of them by the child himself and to guard against didacticism. At the same time, Adler supports the elimination of many tales such as "The Wolf and the Seven Little Kids" because of distrust, violence, fear and attention to ancient religions.

197. Aitken, Johan L. "The Tale's the Thing: Northrop Frye's Theory Applied to the Teaching of Tales in the Elementary School." Interchange 7(1976-1977): 63-72.

198. Allen, Arthur T. "The Ethos of the Teller of Tales." Wilson Library Bulletin 40(1965): 356-358.

In a world flooded with multi-media materials, Allen feels far too many teachers are attempting to teach reading to children who have never experienced the magic of language that storytelling and folk tales share. "When one listens to a story, one is being creative himself, he is adding to it with his own imagination." Through these experiences with folk tales of language and imagination children are more able to become

dreamers and creators. All who share tales with child-
ren--be they parents, teachers or storytellers--also
create for the child a sense of culture and tradition
to which he was born.

199. Anderson, William. "Fairy Tales and the Elementary
Curriculum or 'The Sleeping Beauty' Reawakened." Elementary
English 46(1969): 563-569.

Believing that folk tales will play an increasing role
in relation to creating quality teaching materials,
Anderson explores "The Sleeping Beauty" as an excellent
example of how a tale may initiate a child's literary
perception. A teacher who is able to unfold the richness of fairy tales to his students is opening the
doors for the rest of the child's literary experiences
and perceptions.

200. Anderson, William and Groff, Patrick. "Myth, Childhood and Culture." In A New Look at Children's Literature.
Belmont, California: Wadsworth Publishing, 1972.

As myths define one's culture, they play a vital role in
the socialization of children. It is most important
"to be developing the intellect of the child to perceive,
enjoy, and experience the vast store of narrative and
image available to him in the mythologies of the
world."

201. Bailey, Carolyn Sherwin. "The Instinct Story." In
For the Story Teller. Springfield, Mass.: Milton Bradley,
1916.

The use of the right tales at the proper time can extend
a child's instinctual feelings for nature, rhythm and
self-preservation. Most especially, the ethical tale
must be carefully chosen with a strong and understand-
able moral, yet one that is veiled.

202. Bailey, Carolyn Sherwin. "Stimulating the Emotions
By Means of a Story." In For the Story Teller. Springfield,
Mass.: Milton Bradley, 1916.

Through tales children experience a variety of emotions
while they are caught up in the magic of story. "The
story which a child feels is going to be a force in his
emotional development."

203. Bailey, Carolyn Sherwin. "Story Telling an Aid to
Verbal Expression." In For the Story Teller. Springfield,
Mass.: Milton Bradley, 1916.

When shared with young children, tales can greatly enhance their language development. Tales are excellent
covert English lessons with their repetition and rich
verbal images. Selection and presentation are vital
to this teaching process via folk tales.

204. Bailey, Carolyn Sherwin. "The Story With Sense Appeal." In For the Story Teller. Springfield, Mass.: Milton Bradley, 1916.

The child's world is filled with new senses and related awarenesses. Children are most often drawn to tales with a strong sense of see, taste, smell or hearing. "The Gingerbread Boy's" big appeal "is to the child's sense of taste." Tales rich with these sensory images work to strengthen children's imaginations.

205. Bailey, Carolyn Sherwin. "Training a Child's Memory By Means of a Story." In For the Story Teller. Springfield, Mass.: Milton Bradley, 1916.

Bailey discusses the process of memory and story, and sees storytelling as a short cut in teaching. Yet, if a tale is to be remembered and become a valuable part of a child's life, it must be a tale with a well defined theme.

206. Bailey, W. L. "Fairy Tales as Character-Builders." Libraries 31(1926): 44-46.

Folk tales are all tales of life and include much of the oldest wisdom of mankind. As they grow and develop their character, these tales have much to offer if the child is receptive. Tales are "no mere theories or fancies about life and the world; they are the fruit of experience..." They cultivate in the child a faith in himself and the world.

207. Bard, Therese Jeanne Bissen. The Effects of Developmental Level, Adult Intervention, Sex and Reading Ability on Response to Four Filmed Versions of Explanatory Folk Tales. Doctoral dissertation, University of Washington, 1977.

Films of explanatory folk tales were found of interest and comprehension to children ages ten and younger, but adolescents found them "childish." Films shown without any intervention and introduction by adults were as well received and understood as those with introductions and intervention.

208. Baruch, Dorothy. "This Question of Fairy Tales." Progressive Education 9(1932): 364-369.

Baruch believes upmost caution should be used in sharing folk and fanciful tales with the very youngest children. Make-believe is wanted with young children only as long as it does not promote confusion between fact and fancy.

209.   Batalla, Benjamin C.   "The Importance of Storytelling
to Growing Children."   The Phillippine Educator, December
1957, pp. 58-59.

Batalla criticizes those teachers who fail to tell
stories to their students and lists numerous benefits
of folk literature and storytelling.   Feeling that
stories well told long outlast lessons and preachings,
Batalla urges teachers to use follow-up activities and
ask questions such as: "Why do you like the story?" or
have students write new endings for the stories they
have been told.

210.   Baudouin, Charles.   "Father Christmas."   In Contemp-
orary Studies, translated from the French by Eden and
Cedar Paul.   1924.   Reprint.   Freeport, New York: Books for
Libraries Press, 1969.

The author confronts the charge that storytelling is
the sharing of lies by defining fairy tales as a work
of art and of truth.   They are as real and as truthful
as our dreams.   Storytelling is presented as a vital
element in a cnild's aesthetic education and requires
the soul of the poet and artist.

211.   Bauman, Richard.   The Development of Competence in
the Use of Solicitational Routines: Children's Folklore and
Informal Learning.   Austin: Southwest Educational Development Lab, 1976.

212.   Beard, Patten.   "Why Banish the Fairy Tale?"
Libraries 34(1929): 457-459.

Beard urges the frequent exposure of children to fairy
tales and feels that while the child of the twenties
was well educated in the realities of science he was
lacking in the realities of fairy tales.   He stresses
fairy tales over folklore for the latter needs a maturity of foreign customs.   The beauty and truth of fairy
tales should be the child's from the start.

213.   Beck, Josephine Bristol.   "Fairy Tales: a Colorful
Activity Your Children Could Do."   Grade Teacher, March
1942, pp. 32-34.

After reading "Jack and the Beanstalk" to her class she
had her students create their own beanstalk and in
time objects from other tales.   The process of bringing
to physical life these tales used many skills including
measuring, arithmetic, reading and writing.

214.   Bingham, Jane, and Scholt, Grayce.   "The Great Glass
Slipper Search: Using Folktales With Older Children."
Elementary English 51(1974): 990-998.

As a means of getting older children interested in folk tales the authors worked with their students in classifying tales by way of type and motif. By using tales such as "Cinderella" that have variants around the world, students became aware of basic cultural traits and differences as they read and compared folk tales.

215. Bino, Marial. "NLW Teenage Troubadours." Wisconsin Library Bulletin 59(1963): 137-138.

Groups of high school students performed as storytellers in local schools and libraries to great success. Both the tellers and younger listeners gained much satisfaction from the endeavor.

216. Blos, Joan. "Traditional Nursery Rhymes and Games: Language Learning Experiences for Preschool Blind Children." New Outlook for the Blind 68(1974): 268-275.

Folk rhymes and stories are excellent literature for sharing with young blind children. Rather than using picture books without the pictures, Blos encourages the use of folk literature which can be shared orally as it was designed and shared intact.

217. Bodger, Andrew. "Folklore: a Source for Composition." College Composition and Communication, October 1975, pp. 285-288.

Bodger views folklore as a rich resource for students of writing. Compositions drawn from folk literature have a greater potential audience in addition to the student's exposure to the humanistic values of folklore. Bodger offers direction for those wishing to have students explore folk literature.

218. Boyd, Gertrude. "Folk Tales for International Understanding." Peabody Journal of Education, September 1949, pp. 90-93.

Boyd, while discussing the leading characteristics of various folk cultures, encourages the sharing of tales from all nations with children. Through these tales children will encounter people of different nations engaged in all facets of life. Folk literature shared is an aid to tolerance and the understanding of others.

219. Bradley, J. B. "The Listening Heart." Wilson Library Bulletin 37(1963): 677-679.

Through sharing folk tales with children a sense of mutual trust may be established between teller and child. By telling tales, one shares many elements about which children think and dream--of what they wish and believe. This sharing of imagination is as related to science as the fine arts.

220.   Brewster, Paul G.   "The Folklore Approach in School
Teaching."   School and Society, 10 February 1951, pp. 85-87.

Brewster encourages the use of local folk literature and
lore throughout the curriculum as a means of following
Dewey's directive of beginning to teach where one finds
his students mentally.   Folklore will provide such a
common base.   While the oral should always be paramount,
folk literature can be found and shared in a variety of
media.

221.   Briggs, Nancy E.   "Rhetorical Dimensions of the
Nursery Rhyme."   Speech Teacher 22(1973): 215-220.

The author discusses the utilization of nursery rhymes
in elementary grade speech units.   Rhymes already
familiar to the child are easier to share orally, thus
reducing fears.   The repetition aids and strengthens
memory development as well.   Counting, social condi-
tioning and history are also inherent in many of the
rhymes making the process multi-functional.

222.   Brose, Patricia Bernice Dunn.   An Analysis of the
Functioning of Gothic Themes in the Folklore and Writing
of Children in the Second and Fifth Grades. Doctoral
dissertation, University of Nebraska, 1973.

By studying the story creations of elementary children,
Brose found that younger children draw more heavily
on folklore in their writing and telling of scary stories than older children.   In all, she found school
children understand little of traditional attitudes
towards the supernatural and instead derive most information from mass media.   Though they must compete with
mass media, once aware of an interested audience, children create fine and well constructed stories of their
own.

223.   Brown, Gilbert L.   "The Case Against Myths, Folk-
Lore, and Fairy Stories as Basal Reading for Children."
Education, November 1921, pp. 159-165.

Brown attacks the theory that folk tales enhance a
child's imagination and finds little reason for their
being shared with children.   Believing the contemporary
child has nothing in common with ancient civilizations,
Brown sees folk literature as having a place only in
terms of brief amusement in a child's life.   While
children may like such tales, it is no evidence that
the tales are of any value.

224.   Bryant, Margaret M.   "Folklore in the Schools: Folklore in College English Classes."   New York Folklore Quarterly 2(1946): 286-296.

While discussing the attributes of having college students collect folk literature--especially proverbs--Bryant speaks to the relationship of children and their own rhymes. Children clearly have different interests and rhymes at different ages. "Children are logical, they are illogical; they are romantic, they are cynical; but they sing about it. These seemingly simple little rhymes have a more profound significance than merely brightening a child's day." They enrich folklore.

225. Bryant, Sara Cone. "The Purpose of Story-Telling in Schools." In How to Tell Stories to Children. Boston: Houghton Mifflin, 1905.

Fairy tales should be shared with children because they enjoy them and the tales offer a view of "truth through the guize of images." Tales can create a bond between teacher and student for a story's primary message is that of joy.

226. Bryant, Sara Cone. "Some Specific Schoolroom Uses of Storytelling." In How to Tell Stories to Children. Boston: Houghton Mifflin, 1905.

Oral literature has much to offer children learning to read, for it fosters creative expression. As children themselves tell stories, each finds his own distinctive style of manner and expression. Folk literature is also a productive point of departure for art activities.

227. Buchan, Vivian. "Tell Them a Story." Wilson Library Bulletin 28(1953): 187-193.

Buchan explores the values and accomplishments of sharing folk literature with children. Adults are encouraged to share tales orally with their children, both at home and at school. As a means of experiencing elements such as love, curiousity and understanding, folk literature has much to offer children. Once experienced, this wide range of emotions inherent in tales becomes a part of the child.

228. Butler, Helen L. "Storytelling: First of the Communication Arts." Catholic Library World 21(1950): 104-108 and 170-173.

Used with children, folk tales shared orally encourage the learning of reading and provide a common core of experience. The bond between teacher and child is also strengthened through the telling of tales. Butler discusses best ways to select tales as well. The second part of this two-part article consists of a bibliography of materials about storytelling and of tales to tell.

229.   Byers, Nell B.   "Porridge For Goldilocks."   Education
Digest, March 1949, pp. 25-26.

   Byers condemns the use of fairy tales with children
   because of their lack of morality. Both "Jack and the
   Beanstalk" and "Goldilocks and the Three Bears" are
   used as examples of tales filled with such immorality.
   Both characters steal from others and are not punished.

230.   Carlson, Ruth Kearney.   "World Understanding Through
the Folktale." In Folklore and Folktales Around the World,
edited by Ruth Kearney Carlson.   Newark, Delaware: International Reading Association, 1972.

   Through exposure to a variety of folk tales from many
   areas children are able to learn about cultural diffu-
   sion and the folk process.   Such tale sharing also
   enhances aesthetic appreciation for music, visual arts,
   literature and dance.   As the child experiences tales
   well told he begins to understand peoples of different
   times and places.   By sharing folk tales, children may
   "intuitively grasp the better qualities of the human
   spirit."

231.   Castle, E. B.   "African Traditional Education." In
Growing Up in East Africa. London: Oxford University Press,
1966.

   Folk literature formed a vital part of African tribal
   education.   Riddles tested judgment, and myths explained the genesis of man and surroundings.   "These tales,
   told with care and with much repetition, were the
   African child's education in what was often a compli-
   cated and beautiful language.   There were no grammar
   books, no writing; but correctness of speech, so char-
   acteristic of illiterate Africans, was learnt by imi-
   tation of their elders."

232.   Cather, Katherine D.   "The Universal Appeal of the
Story." In Religious Education Through Story-Telling.
New York: Abingdon Press, 1925.

   Cather discusses the long place of story and folk literature in society, most especially as used as a teaching tool.   Stories have been used by all major religious
   leaders as a way of sharing their particular mythology
   and folk literature.   The author also deals with the
   sharing process and its place in work with children.

233.   Chambers, Dewey W.   "Storytelling and the Curriculum."
In Storytelling and Creative Drama. Dubuque: William C.
Brown, 1970.

   A curriculum that does not include oral storytelling
   cannot offer a complete literary education.   Oral

literature provides rich lingual experiences and images.
Storytelling also has much to contribute to social
studies and cultural awareness. Holidays are seen as
a fine point of departure for folk literature programs.

234. Chambers, Dewey W. "Storytelling: the Neglected Art."
Elementary English 43(1966): 715-719.

The storyteller is an important element in any classroom. Folk tales can be used to enrich all sections
of a curriculum and heighten the students' understanding of his cultural heritage and those of others. A
bibliography of folk tales is included.

235. Chaparro, Jacqueline L. "From the Cradle to the
Classroom." Language Arts 56(1979): 256-261.

Nursery rhymes provide an important link between generations and are a significant part of a child's literary heritage. Rhymes can be used in a variety of ways
to enrich language arts programs.

236. Chubb, Percival. "The Value and Place of Fairy
Stories." In Journal of Proceedings and Addresses of the
44th Annual Meeting. National Education Association, 1905.

Chubb believes fairy tales aid the child in the process
of mind over matter and develop a free spirit. Tales
are also art products that give the child universal
poetic truths. As to editions or the telling of tales,
Chubb deplores vocabulary controlled versions and urges
the stories remain fluid and vital with no set form of
language.

237. Chukovsky, Kornei. "The Battle for the Fairy Tale."
In From Two to Five, translated by Miriam Morton. Berkeley:
University of California Press, 1963.

The author relates (originally in 1929) the struggle
to gain acceptance of the fairy tale in the U.S.S.R.
As children denied fairy tales will, out of need, create
their own, it is wise to share the quality folk tales
that are works of art. Tales do a great deal to foster
the imagination whether the child becomes a poet or
scientist. Tales help the child orient himself to his
surrounding world and allow him to participate in a
wide variety of emotional experiences. The goal of
tales shared is to "awaken, nurture, and strengthen in
the responsive soul of the child this invaluable ability to feel compassion for another's unhappiness and to
share in another's happiness--without this man is in-
human." This essay has also been reprinted in Children
and Literature: Views and Reviews, edited by Virginia
Haviland. Glenview, Illinois: Scott, Foresman and Co.,
1973.

238.   Cober, Mary E., and Pierce, Hazel J.   "The Folklore
Way to Understanding a Unit in Eighth-Grade English."
English Journal 43(1954): 191-192.

> Seeing the primary goal of education to be the trans-
> mitting of basic concepts of American life to children,
> the authors promote the utilization of folk literature.
> As folk literature surrounds everyone and exhibits the
> essence of a culture, when exposed to tales children
> absorb their heritage as they develop language and
> writing skills.

239.   Coleman, Mrs. Thomas.   "Storytelling in the Home."
Wisconsin Library Bulletin 24(1928): 132-133.

> Believing folk tales are most suited for children,
> Coleman urges the re-establishment of storytelling in
> the home.   At the same time sharing tales also carries
> the responsibilities of morality and proper grammar.
> Proper selection is paramount.   Tales which hinge on
> trickery or disobedience, such as "Jack and the Beanstalk,"
> should not be told.   Tales that can be questioned as
> to ethics should be avoided.

240.   Colgan, Richard T.   "Tickle Their Imagination."
Peabody Journal of Education, November 1965, pp. 138-144.

> The author discusses judicious selection and sharing of
> fairy tales with children.   Tales have much to offer in
> regard to imagination, communication and social rela-
> tionships.   Tales chosen and shared wisely promote the
> development of a healthy personality.

241.   Connell, Jane.   A Study of Children's Interests in
Fairy Tales.   Doctoral dissertation, New York University,
1898.

242.   Coville, Alice Perkins.   "The Usefulness of Fables and
Folklore in Teaching Kindness and Consideration." Home
Progress 4(1915): 1169-1173.

> Coville praises the richness of folk literature and all
> it has to offer children.   "Folk-lore is the very
> alphabet on which depends the interpretation of liter-
> ature and art.   It is replete with lessons; but imagi-
> nation, fancy, and tenderness are its most valuable
> by-products."   Through every tale a child is told he
> learns another element of fidelity and faith.

243.   Coville, Alice Perkins.   "The Value of Fairy Tales in
the Teaching of Courage."   Home Progress 4(1915): 1123-1126.

> Feeling that legends stand for truths adults have for-
> gotten, Coville encourages their telling to children.
> Tales are active and establish models of virtuous be-
> havior.   "Over and over the fairies teach us that true

fortitude is seen only in the great exploits warranted
by justice and guided by wisdom." Fairy tales are
ladders from youth to age.

244. Cowles, Julia Darrow. "Why Tell Stories in School?"
In The Art of Story-Telling With Nearly Half a Hundred
Stories. Chicago: A. C. McClurg and Co., 1916.

Through telling tales a teacher may become much closer
to his students via the experiences shared. Stories
told can restore order to a classroom, aid language
arts, teach values and history, and form a taste for
good literature.

245. Crook, Patricia R. "Folktales Teach Appreciation
For Human Predicaments." Reading Teacher, January 1979,
pp. 449-452.

Crook discusses the presence of human disabilities in
folk tales and children's reactions and perceptions of
such disabilities. Feeling questioning techniques are
important as a way of involving children in tales,
Crook suggests reflective/interpretive questions in con-
junction with the stories. Also recommended are having
children make puppets, write character diaries and in-
terviews. A list of tales that suit such activities
is included.

246. "The Crusade Against Fairy Tales." Current Opinion
72(1922): 87-88.

A report on Montessori's controversial opinion that
fairy tales are morbid, pathological and deadly as well
as fostering mental confusion is examined in this essay.
Countering this philosophy is A. Van Gennep who believes
fairy tales enhance imagination and sharpen the child's
inner eye to see more clearly.

247. Crutcher, Frances. "Let Them Live Those Rhymes!"
Instructor, March 1976, p. 109.

Crutcher relates her classroom experiences of having
children recite and then act out familiar rhymes. Such
an activity allows all students oral expression and
developes their imaginations.

248. Cummings, Ella. "Should They Believe in Fairies?"
Grade Teacher, February 1954, p. 47.

Cummings feels that the fairy tale can justify itself
by way of educational results. The stories are filled
with elemental truths and help children understand
others. The author closes by providing an educational
outline for the use of "King Midas."

249. Curtis, David. "With Rhyme and Reason." Language Arts 52(1975): 947-949.

Nursery rhymes provide an excellent introduction to poetry in upper elementary grades. Rhymes demonstrate the relationship of poem to metaphor and object. By exploring the history of rhymes the child becomes well aware that a poem means much more than it actually says.

250. Deasey, Denison. "Literary and Social Class: France." In Education Under Six. New York: St. Martin's Press, 1978.

Deasey briefly discusses the place of fairy tales in the maternelles of France and the challenge of Montessori's attack on tales by Andre Mareuil of the University of Tours. Alain and Van Gennep are also listed as supporters of fairy tales in schools during the 1930s. The author questions of what equal richness can be found to replace folk tales in those schools rejecting them.

251. Depres, Nancy. A Critical Appraisal of the Writings of Educators, Psychologists and Librarians on the Value of Fairy Tales for Children. Master's thesis, Bank Street College of Education, 1958.

252. Dickinson, Sarah. "Storytelling is Fairy Gold." Instructor, November 1961, pp. 81-82.

In this brief article, Dickinson discusses folk tales as being useful in teaching history, biography and character. Storytelling entertains, inspires, enlarges a child's experiences, trains memory and even exposes sham.

253. Dickinson, Sarah, and Others. "Storytelling Magic: Western Style." Top of the News, May 1963, pp. 7-11.

Dickinson supports the idea of a traveling storyteller visiting area schools so that children's imaginations are stretched in this world of electric audio-visual devices. A folk tale well told aids a child's conception of a foreign land better than any encyclopedia can do.

254. Dinkel, Robert M. "The Influence of Nursery Literature on Child Development." Sociology and Social Research 31(1947): 285-290.

Dinkel views the connection of fantasy and imagination as an error and urges the abandonment of traditional tales. Not only do they confuse, they cause fear by the large number of animals that populate them. He suggests parents find stories "pertinent to the child's culture, particularly to the commonplace activities of his family and community."

255. Dodd, Catherine I. "Fairy Tales in the Schoolroom."
Living Age, 8 November 1902, pp. 369-375.

256. Dohrmann, Irma. An Analysis of the Grimm Folk Tales
in Versions Designed For Children. Master's thesis,
University of Chicago, 1951.

257. Dzobo, N. K. "Values in Indigenous African Education."
In Conflict and Harmony in Education in Tropical Africa,
edited by Godfrey Brown and Mervyn Hiskett. Rutherford:
Dickinson University Press, 1976.

> While values are taught in a variety of ways, many are
> embodied in folk literature which is shared time and
> time again. The values and lessons are taught by fami-
> liarizing the children with the myths and legends. Pro-
> verbs, as well, establish values and opinions relative
> to the mores of the culture at hand.

258. Eaton, Edythe N. The Use of Fairy Tales and Folk
Tales as a Teaching Technique in the Primary Grades.
Master's thesis, Allegheny College, 1955.

> The author told a series of fifty fairy tales during
> the second semester to twenty-six third graders. The
> tales were told without preplanned questions or related
> activities. On occasion students discussed a tale out
> of their own curiosity. When compared, stories the
> children wrote after exposure to fairy tales were better
> written, longer and more descriptive than those composed
> before the experiment. Eaton views this as clear sup-
> port for the telling of fairy tales to children and
> varifies their influence on language development and
> imagination as well as affecting greater self initia-
> tive, organization of thoughts and establishment of
> ideals.

259. Eliasberg, Ann P. "Once Upon a Bedtime." New York
Times Magazine, 31 October 1965, p. 129.

> The author, with the help of Ellin Greene via an inter-
> view, suggests parents spend time telling stories to
> their children on an informal basis. A parent who
> shares tales with his child is helping the child stretch
> his capacities for all emotions.

260. Elizabaray, Alga Marina. "Speech" In Give Children
the Best. International Conference of Writers and Theoreticians of Literature for Children and Young People.
Dobris, Czechoslovakia, 1975.

> Elizabaray views the fairy tale as a work of art and
> believes they carry initial truths. Not only do they
> prepare children for reading, tales shape aesthetic
> notions and allow a finer expression of emotions via a
> richer vocabulary.

261. "Fairy Tales and Folk Stories: the Significance of Multicultural Elements in Children's Literature." Reading, December 1978, pp. 10-21.

262. Farr, T. J. "Some Uses of Folklore in Teaching English." Peabody Journal of Education, January 1940, pp. 260-262.

Folk literature offers much to the teaching of English. Language studies can be sparked by riddles and proverbs just as complete tales encourage imagination. The use of folk literature allows the fusing of English to other disciplines such as social studies. Farr concludes with "The emphasis upon folklore should in no sense supplant the study of artistic or classic literature, but should aid in giving students an appreciation of their language and literature and in stimulating them to creative effort."

263. Flaumenhaft, A. S. "Children's 'Sick' Stories." Educational Forum 33(1969): 473-477.

The author criticizes a variety of folk tales for their violence, lack of logic and immorality. Flaumenhaft feels strongly that such tales should be kept away from children. "We want our children to grow up to be not brutalized but civilized men and women...To this end, let us offer them reading matter that will cultivate their finest potentialities, that will make them happier and healthier minded citizens of tomorrow." Tales criticized include "The Three Little Pigs" "Henny Penny," "Little Red Riding Hood," "Half Chick," "Clever Elsie," "The Gingerbread Boy," and "Snow White."

264. Forbes, Cheryl. "What Tall Tales Teach." Christianity Today, 21 January 1977, p. 22.

While factual information is important, the folk tales shared in classrooms teach more about countries and cultures' imaginations. Forbes describes five recent collections of tales that are of fine quality.

265. Forbush, William Byron. "Stories and School." In Manual of Stories. Philadelphia: George Jacobs, 1915.

The tale well told has much to offer organized education. Folk literature may be used to help and introduce creative thinking, literature, history, nature study as well as mores. "It encourages and brightens the dullard; it cheers the pessimist or the discouraged pupil; it helps the introspective one to look outside himself; it soothes the nervous child, and it steadies the unstable."

266.   Forbush, William Byron.   "Stories in the Home." In
Manual of Stories. Philadelphia: George Jacobs, 1915.

Comfort and companionship are two major beneficial elements of folk literature shared in the home.   As
opposed to school settings, tales told in the home can
be selected for the individual child.   Above all other
times, bedtime is one of the finest and most magical
for sharing folk tales.

267.   Forbush, William Byron.   "The Story in Character
Building: Imaginative Stories."   In Manual of Stories.
Phildelphia: George Jacobs, 1915.

Forbush believes a child's exposure to stories should
evolve as he ages, beginning with tales stressing sensory appeal through the various genres of folk literature before sharing realistic stories.   As he discusses
the various forms of stories, the author offers an
example of most forms.

268.   Forbush, William Byron.   "The Value of Storytelling."
In Manual of Stories. Philadelphia: George Jacobs, 1915.

The author discusses the multiple values of folk literature and storytelling which includes the educational,
physical and emotional.   Its place in character building is three-fold for tales shared orally aid a child
in knowing what is good, for him to want what is good,
and to feel what is good.   Tales shared must be related directly to life.

269.   Forseth, Sonia.   "Cinderella, Shave Off Your
Mustasche."   Language Arts 53(1976): 172-174.

Forseth urges the use of folk tales for creative dra-
matics because of their sound structure, adventure,
characters and morals.   If there are more children than
characters, Forseth advises the creation of other parts
or borrowing from Disney films for ideas.

270.   Frank, Josette.   "Fairy and Folk Tales and Other
Fantasy." In Your Child's Reading Today. rev. ed. Garden
City, New York: Doubleday, 1969.

Frank feels the place of fantasy in children's literature is secured.   Fairy tales provide the child escape,
wishfulfillment and a base of familiar faces and situations for his own fantasy life.   The height of fairy
tale interest comes at age eight and care should be
taken so has not to frighten the very young.

271.   Freidson, Eliot Lazarus.   Myth and the Child: an
Aspect of Socialization. Master's thesis, University of
Chicago, 1950.

272.   Froebel, Friedrich.   "Narration of Stories and Leg-
ends, Fables and Fairy Tales. Etc." In The Education of
Man, translated by W. N. Hailmann.   1885. Reprint. New
York: Augustus M. Kelly, 1970.

   Froebel sees the child attracted to the legend and fairy
   tale by the tales' spiritual life that allows the child
   a glance at his own life.   "Every story seems to him
   a new conquest, a fresh treasure; and whatever it
   shows and teaches he adds to his own life for his
   advancement and instruction."

273.   Futz, Dessa M.   "Storytelling as a Morale-Builder
for Children." Recreation, May 1943, pp. 74-75.

   Futz sees storytelling as entertainment for children,
   but also as character-building and a source of inspiration.   During World War II when more children than
   ever were in group care centers, storytelling could
   offer encouragement in a warring world.

274.   Galbraith, Ruth Budd.   "Storytelling: a Wartime
Activity."   Wilson Library Bulletin 17(1943): 723.

   During the war years when more children were in day
   care centers storytelling experienced a revival.   Galbraith encourages storytelling not only for its entertainment value, but for its covert ways of stimulating
   the "imagination toward braver deeds and higher ideals"
   and literary enrichment.

275.   Geboe, Juanita.   "Folklore For Superior Readers in
Third Grade."   Elementary English 37(1960): 93-97.

   In a survey of folk literature with third graders it
   was found that myths were most popular and of the folk
   tales "Snow White" and "The Hare and the Tortoise" were
   favorites.   The survey involved the sharing of tales
   via radio, tape, records and reading, but not telling.

276.   Godfrey, Elizabeth.   "Nursery Lore." In English
Children in the Olden Times. 1907. Reprint. Williamstown,
Mass.: Corner House, 1980.

   Acknowledging the "uneducated" child's nurse as the most
   important character in a child's first education, Godfrey
   discusses the many rhymes, riddles and verbal puzzles
   which have long formed the basis of English language
   acquisition.   Such folk literature has gone beyond the
   nursery to permeate all areas of literature including
   plays by Shakespeare.

277.   Goldsmith, Sadie.   The Place of the Fable in Moral
Education. Doctoral dissertation, New York University,
1936.

278. Grey-Theriot, John Milton. The Folk Tale as an Art
Literature and Its Effect Upon the Emotion and Imagination
of the Child. Master's thesis, Carnegie Institute of
Technology, 1950.

279. Haley, Gail. "Caldecott Award Acceptance." Horn
Book 47(1971): 363-368.

   Haley discusses the educational role of the traditional
   African storyteller and the need for a return to oral
   sharing of tales in the United States that is so dom-
   inated by television. Oral sharing of tales aids a
   child's language and questioning skills. "The give-and-
   take between storyteller and child was a vital educational experience. It provided incentives for speech
   and for self-expression."

280. Hambly, W. D. "Folk Lore as a Factor in Moral Train-
ing." In Origins of Education Among Primitive Peoples: a
Comparative Study in Racial Development. 1926. Reprint.
New York: Negro University Press, 1969.

   Hambly discusses the place of folk literature and storytelling in the education of children in a variety of
   cultures including Nigeria and Ainu. Sections of tales
   are related to show specific behavioral and moral lessons the children are meant to absorb. Each culture's
   stories stress beliefs most important to them including
   respect for the elderly, courage and perseverance.

281. Hannan, Loretta. The Fables, Fairy and Folk Tales in
Second-Grade Readers. Master's thesis, George Washington
University, 1937.

282. Haring, Lee, and Foreman, Ellen. "Folklore in the
Freshman Writing Course." College English 37(1975): 13-21.

   In an effort to aid students in developing writing skills
   the authors discuss the numerous ways folk literature
   may be used. By examining their own oral literature
   students will come to hear their language and by collecting lore they will come to trust their own observations and writing.

283. Haslam, Gerald. "American Oral Literature: Our Forgotten Heritage." English Journal 60(1971): 709-723.

   Using numerous samples of traditional oral literature
   (including Black and Amerindian cultures) Haslam discusses the vital place of such tales in working with
   children. Folk verse and songs are also examined for
   the viable and valuable place they deserve in school
   programs. Oral prose serves as a fine tool in altering
   ones misconceptions about other cultures because the
   tales reflect the people rather than tell about them.

284.   Hetherington, J. Newby. "The Use of Fairy Tales in
the Education of the Young." In A Peculiar Gift: Nineteenth
Century Writings on Books for Children, edited by Lance
Salway. Harmondsworth, England: Kestrel, 1976.

Seeing fairy tales as always popular with "right-minded"
children, the author in 1897 feels tales are important
to the development of one's whole nature. Tales show
the beauty of life to children as opposed to the sci-
ences. Children also gain via tales in regard to memory and attention. Those who are nurtured on fairy
tales will then learn to delight in other literature.
This essay was originally published in The Journal of
Education 19(1897)

285.   Hettiger, Doris. "Storytelling Experiment." School
Library Journal, May 1973, pp. 49-50.

Middle school students under the author's directions
learned and shared folk literature with elementary
children. Children, faculty and administrators were
pleased with the outcome. Hettiger outlines the group's
class sessions and steps taken to learn the art of
storytelling. This essay was originally printed in
Wisconsin Library Bulletin, September-October 1972.

286.   Heuscher, Julius E. "Folklore in Education." In
A Psychiatric Study of Myths and Fairy Tales: Their Origin,
Meaning and Usefulness. Springfield, Illinois: Charles C.
Thomas, 1974.

The child finds in folk literature a world more real
than that explained by science. Interaction between
the child and stories affirms the child's self respect,
self awareness and enables him to grow towards a life
richer than that of pragmatic everyday life.

287.   Higgins, James. "Traditional Literature: Roots of
Philosophy." Social Studies 69(1978): 258-264.

Higgins discusses the multiple riches of folk literature
and the many elements it offers children. While tales
have much to share, they do not "teach" or lecture. Instead, they offer the child a sense of place within
nature and life's events. Higgins also counters charges
against violence in tales and those who feel tales are
only for young children. "Like philosophers, storytellers are constantly engaged in the ancient activity
of wondering aloud."

288.   Hill, May. "Place of the Folk Tale Today." Childhood Education, November 1931, pp. 123-128.

Hill approaches the subject of children and folk literature with guarded enthusiasm. Believing that most
folk literature is for adults, she encourages careful
selection of tales shared and offers suggestions for
ways of best sharing them. Contemporary tales of realism also have their valuable place and should be balanced with tales of fancy.

289. Hill, Ruth A. "Storytelling Around the World: a
Symposium. Part I. United States." Library Journal, 1 April
1940, pp. 285-289.

After Marie Shedlock's initial visits to the United
States, the use of storytelling and folk literature
with children became a regular element of library
services.

290. Hoffman, Mary. "Missing Out On Folklore." Times
Educational Supplement, 8 February 1974, p. 61.

Hoffman discusses the phenomenon of so many contemporary children not being aware of the traditional tales
of their heritage be the tales Ulysses or "Little Red
Riding Hood." Feeling that the telling of folk tales
to children is a vital part of education, the author
describes in brief different methods of telling and
resources for those who wish to learn.

291. Hotchkiss, Mary. "Storytelling in the Kindergarten."
In Proceedings of the International Congress of Education
of the World. Columbian Exposition 1893. Under the Charge
of the N.E.A. National Education Association. 32(1893):
351-355.

Hotchkiss sees fairy tales as certainly being for children and as "The early race was educated by myths and
legends...each child follows the development of the
race." Still, caution must be observed so as not to
tell tales with negative endings or in impure English.
Tales of imagination can aid the child in seeing the
beauty of his surroundings.

292. Hoyt, Howard. "Violence in Children's Folk Tales."
PTA Magazine, January 1974, pp. 26-27.

Having had a child in a creative drama exercise attempt
to literally poke out the Trolls eyes in "The Three
Billy Goats Gruff," Hoyt addresses the possible effects
of violence in folk tales. It must be remembered that
most tales were originally for adults. To discard the
tales, however, would be a loss. Hoyt recommends careful selection for when "Introduced to children at the
proper age level, say eight or nine,...the folktale
provides an appetizer to history." If shared well,
tales can make a positive contribution to a child's
education.

293. Hughes, Ted. "Myth and Education." In Writers,
Critics and Children, edited by Geoff Fox and Others.
New York: Agathon Press, 1976.

   Hughes exaimines Plato's idea that the proper education
   for ideal citizens is to be found in traditional tales
   and myths. As children hear and take possession of
   tales they begin to work with images and the words
   which represent them. The child can return to any por-
   tion or image of the tale by calling up the needed
   word and in turn story fragments become such "words"
   for the entire tale. A primary example of this is that
   any tale fragment of Christ brings to mind the entire
   story of his life and work. An earlier and slightly
   different version of this essay was printed in Children's Literature in Education, March 1970.

294. Hull, Barbara Ann. An Examination of Selected Editions of Folklore for Children. Master's thesis, Western
Michigan University, 1968.

295. Jackson, Dan. "Teaching Ancient Myths and Their
Modern Counterparts." Media and Methods, September 1978,
pp. 45-46.

   Jackson describes and discusses his high school class
   on mythology. Students explored both classical tales
   and contemporary media tales such as Star Trek, Summer-
   hill and West Side Story. Also examined were fairy
   tales and the concerns of violence, sorrow and death.
   A bibliography of suggested materials is included.

296. Jennette, Louise S. The Fairy Tale in a Realistic
World. Master's thesis, North Carolina Agriculture and
Technical College, 1959.

297. Johnson, E. D. "Storytelling as an Aid in Child
Development." Primary Education--Popular Education,
December 1928, pp. 290-291.

298. Jones, Mercedes. The Didactic Element and the Poetic
Justice in Fairy Stories. Master's thesis, University of
Idaho, 1926.

299. "Killing the Fairies." Literary Digest, 24 March 1923,
p. 31.

   Countering anti-fairy tale statements by Montessori and
   others, this essay offers arguments in favor of the
   value of fairy tales. A primary reason of support is
   the child's want and need of such tales. Without traditional tales children will create their own savage
   realistic tales to fill the void.

300. Klee, Loretta E. "Folklore and the Development of Critical Thinking." Social Education 10(1946): 267-269.

Klee reports on the use of folk literature and folk research with junior high students. Through their collecting of local tales and lore students developed many elements of critical thinking and reasoning. The students' findings were presented to the local library so all could share in their heritage.

301. Korpalski, Adam. "The Case for Folk Literature." Todays Education, November 1970, p. 63.

Korpalski urges the inclusion of folk literature in the school curriculum and briefly describes a class in folklore at his school. Both storytelling and listening skills were emphasized.

302. Kready, Laura Fry. "The Worth of Fairy Tales." In A Study of Fairy Tales. Boston: Houghton Mifflin, 1910.

Kready finds great worth in fairy tales for they bring to a child's life joy, feed his play spirit, aid his social development and strengthen powers of imagination and language. Differing from Montessori, Kready feels tales improve one's study of nature for they increase visualization and the ability to see and reflect.

303. Langfeldt, Dr. J. "The Educational and Moral Values of Folk and Fairy Tales." In Suitable for Children, edited by Nicholas Tucker. Berkeley: University of California Press, 1976.

The author covers a variety of past opinions regarding folk tales ranging from Rousseau to De Greff. Finding himself on middle ground, Langfeldt supports some tales such as "Star Money" and "The Water of Life" yet condemns others including "Hansel and Gretel" and "Cinderella." This essay was originally printed in The Junior Bookshelf, January 1961.

304. Lee, Hector H. "American Folklore in the Secondary Schools." English Journal 59(1970): 994-1004.

Lee explores three basic ways folklore (tales, jokes, beliefs, etc.) can be used with school children: (1)teaching units, (2)support material for motivation and (3)entertainment. Folk literature gives significance to one's immediate environment, clarifies one's own culture, increases awareness of values and commonalities of other cultures and helps the student develop a sense of the worth of the common man.

305. Lemon, Joyce P. "The Child's Need for Myths and Legends in the Mother Tongue." School Librarian 20(1972): 102-106.

Children deprived of myths and folk tales frequently end up in slower classes for they have much less to draw on in terms of language and emotional experiences. Lemon sees that "Neglect of myth, legend and folktale among slaves sent out from Africa during the nineteenth century is partly responsible for the bitterness among Black Americans today."

306. Levin, Beatrice S. "Storytelling in Religious Education." Catholic School Journal, September 1966, pp. 63-64.

Through folk literature and storytelling a teacher may encourage reflective thinking in children and create a hunger for better things as well as develop their imagination. Tales, especially religious ones, can "imbue in the child a desire to act in a socially acceptable way and to serve humanity."

307. Lewis, Claudia. "Fairy Tales and Fantasy in the Classroom." Childhood Education, November 1972, pp. 64-67.

Lewis reports on a multi-school experiment in which teachers read folk tales and fantasies to their students for a two month period. Children were urged to respond via drawing, music, theater, or writing. It was found that time and again the stories mirrored concerns of the children and emotional growth was affected.

308. Lips, Julius E. "Education Without Books." In The Origin of Things. New York: Fawcett, 1956.

The author explores the form and methods of education before the printed world. In such times and cultures folk literature and folklore in general were the education of all and on an equal level. Stories served as religion, history and ethics.

309. Locke, John. John Locke on Education, edited by Peter Gay. New York: Teachers College, Columbia University Press, 1964.

As a child begins to read Locke urges care in the selection of reading material so as not to fill his head with "perfectly useless trumpery; or lay the principles of vice and folly." Locke's two examples of acceptable books are the folk literature editions Aesop's Fables and Reynard the Fox which he views as entertaining to the child and also filled with useful reflections to the adult. Locke's views on folk literature and children first appeared in 1693 in his work entitled Some Thoughts Concerning Education.

310.   Lockwood, Deanna L.   Trends in the Publishing of Folktales for Children in the United States From Colonial Times to the Present.   Master's thesis, University of Chicago, 1972.

Lockwood traces some of the trends of folk tales published for children in the United States since colonial times and examines what influences their publication had on the field of children's literature. History, growth, and changing ethnic make-up of the United States are all reflected in the history of published folk tales for children.

311.   Lollis, Mary Esther.   "The Noodle Story." Elementary English Review 19(1942): 199-200.

As a teacher who works with children of lower IQ's, Lollis finds the "noodle" genre of folk tales most enjoyable and effective.   Such tales are filled with events where the weak outwit the strong and the smart person loses out to the foolish one.   Through these tales children labled as inferior are able to exper- ience vicarious success and laugh at characters in- ferior to themselves.   "The atmosphere of these stories is simple helping to undo the complexities of modern life...They are a deep source of education as they give the child a chance to visit other lands and cultures and absorb the atmosphere found there."   A brief bib- liography is included.

312.   M. Bertilla, Sister.   "The Fairy Tale in the Educa- tion of the Child."   Catholic Educational Review, January 1934, pp. 25-33.

The fairy tale is a poetic presentation of spiritual truths and offers children much in terms of moral development.   They are the heritage of every child and prepare them for other literature.   Yet, while fairy tales have much to offer, adults must guard against "rubbing in their lesson" or trying to rewrite and up- date the stories.   Mother Goose--though she is absurd-- is just what the child likes: humor, nonsense and the imaginative.

313.   MacArthur, James F., and Carr, John C.   "Que Vous Avez de Grandes Oreilles: Instant Foreign Language Through Fairy Tales."   French Review 48(1975): 1005-1008.

MacArthur and Carr encourage the oral telling of fairy tales in French or other languages to classes studying that particular language.   Just as tales in English help English-speaking children develop an ear for language through repitition so does the tale told in French to the French student or in Spanish to the student of Spanish.

314.   McCulley, Ova Bumbalough.   A Study of the Effect of
Fairy Tales on Children in the Primary Grades.   Master's
thesis, Tennessee Polytechnic Institute, 1964.

McCulley examined the various views of educators,
psychologists and parents towards fairy tales and
children in recent times, questioned teachers about
their use of fairy tales and evaluated text books in
regard to number and type of folk tales included.
General opinion accepts fairy tales as being both
popular with children and of value, but some caution
is needed as to what tales are told to what age levels.
It is recommended that if one is bothered by elements
of a particular tale it should not be told rather
than rewritten and watered down.   Fairy tales "provide
an invaluable background for the enjoyment of great
literature in later life.   They help to develop an
understanding of how other people live and think, to
cultivate a sense of humor, and to teach lessons without making a point of it."   Included is a bibliography
of suggested tales for each grade level.

315.   MacDonald, Greville.   "The Fairy Tale in Education."
Living Age 28 June 1913, pp. 783-790.

Viewing fairy tales as as natural and vital as childhood and wild flowers, the author discusses folk
literature as an art form of which children should be
a part.   MacDonald feels the child deserves to be
trusted in his ability to "handle" fairy tales rather
than having them kept from him.   And when shared, it
must be remembered that tales need not have obvious
morals in order to work their magic.

316.   McDowell, John.   "Riddling and Enculturation: a
Glance at the Cerebral Child."   ED 129 433.   1976.

Riddles, a genre of folk literature, serve to sharpen
a child's wit and allows the child lingual experimenta-
tion.   Children learn via riddles to classify, articu-
late and assess language as an arbitrary instrument.

317.   McDowell John Holmes.   The Speech Play and Verbal
Art of Chicano Children: an Ethnographic and Sociolinguis-
tic Study.   Doctoral dissertation, University of Texas at
Austin, 1975.

McDowell collected various genre of folk literature in
Chicano neighborhoods in Austin and analyzes the function of these materials in the enculturation process.
The study examined the ages between four and eleven
during which the child becomes a competent performer
of several folk literature genres.

318. MacLaughlin, Elizabeth Jean Mayo. Peru's Urban
Migrant Children Learn Folktales: Developmental Acquisition of Narrative Skill in a Quecha-Migrant Squatter Settle-
ment in Arequipa. Doctoral dissertation, Indian University, 1977.

    The author examines the changes in folk narratives due
    to age changes and developmental changes of the child
    tellers. It was found that by ages eleven to twelve
    children had mastered most aspects of traditional syn-
    tax and storytelling. One hundred-Ninety-two texts are
    included and age level elements of tale-telling are
    related to other current research.

319. McPherson, Ruth Hale. Analysis of Folklore Material
Found in Elementary Readers. Master's thesis, George
Peabody College, 1931.

320. Majasan, J. A. "Traditional Education and Its
Possible Contribution to Modern Educational Techniques."
West African Journal of Education 19(1975): 423-434.

    One of the primary techniques of traditional education
    is the indirect teaching through folk literature. As
    soon as children are old enough, they are expected to
    join in the night storytelling sessions at which moral
    lessons are drawn and practical conclusions indicated.

321. Maranda, Elli. "Myth and Art as Teaching Materials:
Occasional Paper No. 5." ED 178 392. 1965.

    Maranda outlines the uses and supportive reasons for
    including folk literature and art in a social studies
    curriculum. Children's exposure to myths and tales of
    alien cultures allows them to come to know a wide range
    of peoples and social patterns.

322. Marble, Sarah. "Can the Storyteller Contribute
Anything to Rural Community?" Education 41(1921): 606-609.

    Marble discusses the many agencies that are utilizing
    storytelling and folk literature for their educational,
    moral and social ends. By sharing stories the author
    feels children will be better equipped to meet the
    realities of life and with more understanding. It is
    one of the most effective means of passing on lessons.

323. Martinez, Ernest Alcario. The Effect of Folk Legends
Told in Chicano Spanish on the Attitudes and Comprehension
of Chicano Children. Doctoral dissertation, University
of California--Berkeley, 1977.

    Martinez examined the differences in comprehension of
    third grade Mexican Americans in regard to folk tales
    read in English and in Chicano Spanish. Findings showed

that as a group there was higher comprehension for the
Chicano versions, but the author urges further study
because they exhibited comprehension in both English
and Chicano Spanish.

324. Mary Anna Aurony, Sister. The Value of the Legend
in Literature for Children. Master's thesis, University
of Notre Dame, 1929.

325. Mary Louis Rongione, Sister. The Nursery Rhyme and
Its Literary Tradition. Master's thesis, Villanova University, 1961.

The author discusses in detail the literary history of
the rhymes known as Mother Goose and concludes her
thesis with thoughts on the value of rhymes to children.
"As an aid to teaching children, nursery lore can be
traced to ancient Rome and the early Christian era."
Mother Goose is an excellent introduction to finer
verse and classic literature. The use of rhymes shares
the imagery and joys of words with the developing child.
Beyond this, they can "teach ideals and morals directly
or by implication." The author acknowledges as well,
those who oppose nursery rhymes finding Mother Goose
a cruel and violent woman.

326. Mead, Margaret. Growing Up in New Guinea: a Comparative Study of Primitive Education. New York: William
Morrow, 1930. pp. 125-126.

Among the Manus, storytelling and literature of fancy
were strongly discouraged. Adults feel legends are
for old people and that children dislike legends. The
storytelling habit does not exist for children in this
culture. "And the 'why?' element in children's con-
versation with adults is superseded by the 'what?' and
'where?' questions."

327. Millender, Dharathula H. "Storytelling--a Teaching
Technique." Education 85(1965): 556-561.

A teacher encourages the use of storytelling and folk
tales as   teaching techniques to bring pleasure and/or
illustrate ideas to children. Millender discusses
different types of tales for different age levels and
the avoidance of tales that deal with death, fear or
sarcasm.

328. Miller, George Tasker. "The Modern Use of the Story."
Story-Telling to Live Wire Boys. New York: Dutton, 1930.

Miller finds the use of stories with groups of all boys
to be a most beneficial activity. The camp director
tells tales for reasons that are different than the librarian. Rather than introducing books, Miller uses
tales to entertain, to attract and to interest.

329.   Miller, Nathan.   The Child in Primitive Society.
New York: Bretano's, 1928.   pp. 168-172.

The most common method of transmitting cultural traits
and information on to children in primitive societies
is by folk literature.   Myths, tales and legends tell
of the past and how one must function in that society.
Miller expresses some reservations in that most of this
storytelling is done by mothers who must rely on memory and are often not allowed to hear in full the tales
men tell to one another.   Miller sees this method of
education as informal and lax.

330.   Movogenes, Nancy A., and Cummins, Joan S.   "What Ever
Happened to Little Red Riding Hood? A Study of a Nursery
Tale and Its Language."   ED 132 576.   1976.

This study analyzes the changing language used to tell
"Little Red Riding Hood" in print over the past two-
hundred years.   The researchers conclude that it is
best for children to be exposed to all kinds of oral
literature as printed language is becomming more and
more limited.

331.   Musselman, Virginia.   "Storytelling: Let Storytelling
Become a Part of Every Activity."   Recreation, March 1948.
pp. 561-564.

Musselman cautions people that folk literature and storytelling should not be set aside, but rather shared
continuously through all situations.   Local folklore
and tales should not be forgotten either.   They can add
greatly to a child's immediate world.

332.   Natarella, Margaret A.   "Getting Students Involved
With Collecting Folklore." Language Arts 56(1979): 156-158.

By having children gather and organize their area folklore and literature they come to a greater understanding of their "roots."   The process fosters a variety
of language skills and is rewarding and insightful as
well.

333.   Nebraska Curriculum Development Center. Nebraska
University.   "Folklore in the Elementary School."
ED 045 679.   1968.

Using examples and discussion, the Center offers suggestions for the collecting and examining of children's
play and local folklore.   A bibliography for adults
is included.

334.   Nesbitt, Elizabeth.   "The Art of Storytelling."
Horn Book 21(1945): 439-444.

Storytelling is an art that reveals the common humanity of all men, for folk literature believes in the human spirit. Tales offer children exposure to various cultures, customs, and ideals as well.

335. Nesbitt, Elizabeth. "Hold To That Which Is Good." Horn Book 16(1940): 7-15.

Nesbitt feels storytelling educates by means of stimulation and inspiration. To tie storytelling to the task of getting children to read is to lose much of storytelling's riches.

336. Newland, Mary Reed. "Storytelling." Catholic Library World 45(1973): 31-33.

Storytelling and folk literature share creative experiences with children unlike most modern media. While tales must never be told didactically, their moral values are shared by osmosis. Newland recounts several examples of the lasting memories of children of their storytelling experiences.

337. O'Dell, Felicity Ann. Socialization Through Children's Literature: The Soviet Example. Cambridge: Cambridge University Press, 1978. pp. 8-17.

O'Dell relates the fluctuating Soviet opinion toward fairy tales and those who worked to restore them to children, including Gorky and Chukovsky. In more recent years, fairy tales have gained Soviet acceptance by being educative through their entertainment values. Still, some recommend that "To acquire any educational value they must be discussed with a person skilled in character-education."

338. Omotoso, Sam. "Storytelling: a Cherished Cultural Heritage in Nigeria." Language Arts 55(1978): 724-727.

Omotoso   discusses the teaching values of telling and retelling traditional stories to children. Through traditional tales children learn morals and customs as well as increased lingual abilities.

339. Osband, Helen. "Storytelling in the Speech Curriculum." Elementary English Review 10(1933): 35-37.

Osband deals with the dilemma of whether storytelling techique is as important as the tale itself in working with children. Regardless of technique, storytelling with children is not only an educational device, but one of the creative arts as well.

340. Parker, Edith C. "Storytelling: Its Relation to
Literary Appreciation." Addresses and Proceedings of the
60th Annual Meeting of the N.E.A. National Education
Association. 60(1922): 1016-1017.

Parker believes storytelling's primary objective is
the presentation of the great literature of the world.
As children do not usually select such for themselves,
the storyteller may share classic tales such as the
Odyssey. Tales shared must always be of literary quality for all are a part of the child's future taste in
literature and language.

341. Partridge, Emelyn, and Partridge, George. "Fairy-
Tales." In Storytelling in School and Home. New York:
Sturgis and Walton, 1912.

At the time of this essay, opinion was increasingly in
favor of including fairy tales in schools. Partridge
sees the fairy tale as having religious significance
for it has a religious relationship to the child. The
child believes and the tales stimulate belief in the
supernatural and unseen worlds. "The fairy-tale is
one of the most earnest products of the mind of man..."

342. Partridge, Emelyn, and Partridge, George. "Primitive
Stories." In Storytelling in School and Home. New York:
Sturgis and Walton, 1912.

The primitive (porquoi) tales of many cultures have
much to offer children. They provide a vivid sense of
the ancient forest and kinship with animals as well as
sharing drama. Such stories--including those of humor--
establish the foundations for appreciating literature
of higher cultures.

343. Partridge, Emelyn, and Partridge, George. "The Story
and the Child." In Storytelling in School and Home. New
York: Sturgis and Walton, 1912.

While acknowledging that there are no definite lines
of demarcation, the authors discuss the various forms
of folk literature best suited for different ages of
children. One should look at the tale itself, not the
language in which it is written, when selecting tales
for a specific age level.

344. Partridge, Emelyn, and Partridge, George. "The Story
in Moral Education." In Storytelling in School and Home.
New York: Sturgis and Walton, 1912.

All genres of folk literature may affect the moral education of children. Through tales, children are exposed
to many points of view and absorb the covert lessons of
behavior. Rather than systematic lessons, virtues may
be passed on through the art of the folk tale.

345.   Pilant, Elizabeth. "American Folklore For Remedial
Reading." English Journal 41(1951): 227-228.

The author found folk tales, especially tall tales, well
suited for slow readers. These tales are high in interest and adventure with basic plots and use of language employed.

346.   Pilant, Elizabeth. "Folklore Contributes to the
Curriculum." Educational Leadership 9(1952): 429-433.

Pilant believes a child's local folk literature is an
important part of his education. Tales shared aid
vocabulary, language patterns and folkways. Beyond
English classes, folk literature can also be a sound
element in social studies. It can stretch a child's
concept of the United States beyond major and often
disasterous current events.

347.   Pilant, Elizabeth. "Folklore in the Elementary
School." Instructor, March 1964, p. 7.

The author, fearing a decline in children's knowledge
of folk literature, discusses a variety of genres and
collections that might be well-shared in elementary
schools. Pilant sees folklore as both a highly rewarding and necessary ingredient in the literature of
elementary schools.

348.   Plato. "Censorship of Literature For School Use."
In The Republic of Plato, translated by Francis MacDonald
Cornford. London: Oxford University Press, 1941.

While recommending folk literature be a primary element
in a child's education, Plato sees the first order of
business as being to supervise the selecting of tales
to be told/shared and the rejecting of all those which
are unsatisfactory. Stories that are "ugly and immoral" or those of warfare and intrigue between the
gods should be excluded. "A child cannot distinguish
the allegorical sense from the literal, and the ideas
he takes in at that age are likely to become indelibly
fixed; hence the great importance of seeing that the
first stories he hears shall be designed to produce the
best possible effect on his character."

349.   Pomeroy, Sally A.   Folklore: Its Use as an Integral
Part of the Elementary Classroom in New York. Master's
thesis, Syracuse University, 1957.

350.   Powers, Mabel. "Storytelling." Elementary English
25(1948): 308-310.

When sharing folk tales with children, the primary function should be joy--the beauty of the spirit. Moral
and ethical instruction are inherent and should not be
stressed.

351. Pressler, Joan. "Storytelling Project for Slow
Learners." A.L.A. Bulletin, February 1963, pp. 168-169.

Folk tales and storytelling were found to be a fine
source of literature for children with reading difficulties. Tales also aided in social studies and created
interest in new subjects among students.

352. Pusey, Mary B. "Storytelling as a Means of Directing
Language Power in the Primary Grades." Virginia Journal
of Education, October 1934, pp. 32-33.

Pusey believes the story is a natural means for in-
structing little children. Tales cultivate imagination, attention span, memory and create a yearning for
good literature.

353. Putnam, John. "Folklore: a Key to Cultural Understanding." Educational Leadership 21(1964): 363-368.

By utilizing folk literature and folklore in all areas
of the curriculum, children will be better able to
understand universal human characteristics. This is in
addition to finding greater meaning in their own lives.
Putnam warns against oversimplification and idealiza-
tion when sharing folklore with children.

354. Putnam, John. "Folklore and Human Relations in the
Elementary School." National Elementary Principal,
April 1961, pp. 14-17.

Putnam investigates various ways folklore and folk
literature can be used by teachers to enrich their
teaching. Shared appropriately, such tales and materials can aid children in understanding various cultures, social experiences and in learning to think
objectively.

355. Raum, O. F. Chaga Childhood: a Description of Indigenous Education in an East African Tribe. International African Institute: Oxford University Press, 1940.

While Raum includes no single section concerning tales
and children, if one reads pages indexed under "Stories,
children and" they will find an aggregate description
of the primitive child and tales--especially in regard
to educational aspects.

356. "The Revival of Storytelling." Literary Digest, 12
July 1913, p. 58.

Drawing from an essay by George Partridge in The Storyteller's Magazine, this article discusses folk tales
and storytelling as an aesthetic experience for the
child. Folk tales have untold levels of riches to
give to children and are an important method of education.

357. Richard, J. A. "Folklore as an Aid to the Teaching
of History." Texas Outlook, March 1940, pp. 15-16.

Richard urges teachers to toss out dates and battles
and make room for the literature of the common folk in
history classes. Folklore and literature are frequently a better clue to the character and psychology of a
culture than cold memorized facts. Students can also
be actively involved in the discovery of oral history
and literature in their own community.

358. Rietz, Sandra A. "Using Children's Folksongs to
Transition Beginning Readers From the Familiar Structure
of Oral Language to the Structure of Written Language."
ED 142 983. 1976.

Utilization of children's folksongs as children pass
into early readers eases the process of transferring
from an oral to a written language. Folksongs provide basic speech patterns and repetition. They can
be read and sung at the same time thus creating a
more comfortable situation for the beginning reader.

359. Rollins, Charlemae. "Storytelling." Illinois
Libraries 42(1960): 134-137.

The author sees storytelling as designed to primarily
entertain while at the same time developing a child's
imagination and deepening his appreciation of beauty
around him. Storytelling and folk literature are important as a method of introducing good books to children. Rollins closes with suggestions of tales to tell
and ways of telling them.

360. Rollins, Charlemae. "Storytelling: Its Value and
Importance." Elementary English 34(1957): 164-166.

Primarily shared to entertain, storytelling also eases
tensions between students and teachers, transmits ideas,
develops imagination, and aids children in coming to
understand the world around them.

361. Rousseau, Jean-Jacques. Emile or On Education, introduction, translation and notes by Allan Bloom. 1762.
Reprint. New York: Basic Books Inc., 1979. pp. 112-116
and 247-249.

In his famous work on education Rousseau both condemns
and utilizes fables as a teaching tool. The deciding
factor is the age of the child. Rousseau feels children must be told the naked truth for they are not cap-
able of understanding the literary form of the fable.
By telling them to children as enjoyment they are se-
duced by the lie and gain nothing. As support, Rousseau
dissects "The Crow and the Fox" pointing out all

reasons for not telling it to a child. For the adolescent, however, who has lived through mistakes, fables
have much to offer. "The child who has never been de-
ceived by praise understands nothing...But the giddy
young man who has just been the dupe of a flatterer
conceives marvelously that the crow was only a fool."
Yet, even at this age, fables cannot be forced. "If
your pupil understands the fable only with the help of
the explanation, be sure that he will not understand
it even in that way."

362. Russell, Louise. Legendary Narratives Inherited by
Children of Mexican-American Ancestry: Cultural Pluralism
and the Persistence of Tradition. Doctoral dissertation,
Indiana University, 1977.

  Russell studied the function of the telling of legends
  among Chicano grade school children in Greeley, Colo-
  rado. Findings discuss storytelling's effect on the
  children's personal and ethnic identity.

363. Ryan, Calvin T. "Advocate For the Fairies." Elementary English Review 11(1934): 268-271.

  The author supports the theory that storytelling cul-
  tivates the imagination. Tales are unmoral being
  neither moral or immoral. Modern educators use the
  story for the pleasure it gives the child and believe
  that the unmoral story serves the purpose as well as
  the moral tale. Tales are no more wicked, cruel or
  vulgar than a child can be in his actions. It is only
  the adult who worries about such levels of morality.

364. Ryan, Calvin T. "The Oldest Method in All This
World." American Childhood, February 1949, pp. 12-13.

  Ryan supports storytelling and fairy tales as being important to a child's growth. Though not literally
  true, the author defends tales as not being lies for
  the spirit of the tales is very truthful. Quoting Dr.
  Angelo Patri, Ryan suggests a bibliotheraputic use of
  fables.

365. Schneider, Gene A. "Storytelling in the Junior High
School." California School Libraries, May 1967, pp. 5-9.

  Deciding storytelling should not be confined to elementary grades, Schneider began telling folk tales and
  myths in his junior high school classes. It proved
  quite successful with numerous teachers requesting his
  telling services and the students asking for more.

366. Schrank, Jeffrey. "Mythology Today." Media and
Methods, April 1973, pp. 22-30.

Schrank examines the contemporary mythology of sports and television in relation to classic Greek mythology. Just as in the past, young people latch onto heroes of superhuman power and existence. He offers suggestions for the combined study of classical and contemporary mythology.

367. Shanklin, Agnes K. "Adventure in English I: a Cultural Odyssey." English Journal 52(1963): 54-57.

The author describes her wide use of folk literaure in her freshman class. Basing her course of study on the theory that modern culture rests firmly on a foundation of ancient myth and folk literature, her class began with Greek mythology, moved through the Odyssey, ending with fairy tales and ballads. As a way of sharing their readings students did skits, lectures, games and told stories.

368. Shannon, George. "Storytelling and the Schools." English Journal, May 1979, pp. 50-51.

As one of the oldest forms of education and entertainment, folk tales have a great deal to offer all areas of the curriculum. Folk literature provides for the child a strong basis for appreciating fine literature, improves reading, adds human reality to social studies and encourages the child's imagination. Tales also offer, without didactism a level of moral education.

369. Shaw, Spencer. "Storytelling Develops Reading." Instructor, November 1951, pp. 17-18.

Shaw feels one must have a purpose for telling a story-- to fill some personal or social need of the group. Hearing tales told well creates in the child an appreciation for literature and will urge him on to reading proficiency.

370. Sheingold, Karen, and Foundas, Anne. "Rhymes For Some Reasons: Effect of Rhyme on Children's Memory For Detail and Sequence in Simple Narratives." Psychological Reports 43(1978): 1231-1234.

The authors used both prose and verse versions of two stories with twenty-four grade school children and found that an equal number enjoyed both forms. They found no effect by form upon their remembering simple details of the stories, but rhyming enhanced the children's ability to sequence the events of the stories. Verse was found to aid children in the development of sequencing skills

371.   Sherman, John Lee.   "Storytelling With Young Children."   Young Children, January 1979, pp. 20-27.

Using Bettelheim's Uses of Enchantment as a spring-
board, Sherman stresses the need for sharing folk literature orally.   He has found that children who hear
stories begin to tell more stories themselves.   Sherman
offers advice on the sharing of various story forms
such as personal experience and traditional.   The
author also supports the changing of traditional tales
and use of props as a way of enhancing the storytelling.

372.   Simmons, Leo W.   The Role of the Aged in Primitive
Society. New Haven: Yale University Press, 1945.   pp. 98-
102.

In discussing the role of the aged as storytellers,
Simmons also covers the interrelationship of child,
tale and elder.   Children of cultures from the Crow
to the Xosa are taught and entertained with folk tales
their elders pass on to them.   This made for a stronger
tie between generations.   The passing on of tales to
children was/is seen as a vital endeavor and something
the elderly can do when they can no longer hunt, etc.

373.   Sivertz, Chloe.   "Back Yard Storytelling."   Wilson
Library Bulletin 23(1949): 624-625.

In an effort to find activities for parents to share
with their children during the school-free summer
months, the author examined storytelling and found
it to be an excellent answer to the problem.

374.   Spear, Ruth Jane.   Uses of American Folklore in the
Sophomore Literature Program of Dover High School. Master's
thesis, Ohio State University, 1962.

Seeing sophomores as being in mid-maturity, between the
exuberance of childhood and the reasoning of adulthood,
Spear believes folk literature to be a perfect bridge.
Children can explore new emotions and experiences while
sharing the adventure of stories.   Such exposure will
also aid their speaking and writing skills.   Folk literature (both tale and song) is not to be developed as
a lesson, but instead presented as an activity that
can be made a part of the program throughout the year.
A variety of activities utilizing folk literature are
discussed and a bibliography in included.   "High-school
students can profit from a knowledge of American folklore, for through its study they receive not only a
better understanding of American traditions but also
an insight into the interrelatedness of American beliefs, customs, songs, and stories with those of other
countries."

375.   Stahl, Mark B.   "Using Traditional Oral Stories in the English Classroom." English Journal, October 1979, pp. 33-36.

Stahl discusses classroom-tested projects involving folk literature. Students were encouraged to go beyond traditional tales already in print and collect oral tales from family and friends. Through the collecting and sharing of oral tales, students came to better understand story structure and the differences between oral and written language. "Perhaps most important, by stressing the educational value of these oral stories, teachers can instill in students a sense that knowledge brought to school is as valuable as that taken from it."

376.   Starbuck, Edwin, and Others.   Fairy Tale, Myth, and Legend: Volume I.   A Guide to Literature for Character Training.   New York, Macmillan, 1929.

The authors view folk literature and storytelling as a most powerful art because "it involves the interplay of life upon life." With that power comes equal responsibility. As tales come from a more primitive time many of them are unnecessary for contemporary children and others are too fantastic rather than fanciful or vengeful rather than zesty. When shared wisely, the folk tale provides deep moral significance and "makes the whole world kin." The authors offer guidelines for the proper selection of tales and include bibliographies organized by grade level, situations, culture, and indexes by attitudes, author and title

377.   Stewig, John Warren.   "Storyteller: Endangered Species?" Language Arts 55(1978): 339-345.

Stewig urges teachers to tell folk tales to their classes for three basic values: (1)an understanding of the oral tradition, (2)active involvement, and (3)use of music with stories.

378.   Studer, Norman.   "The Place of Folklore in Education." New York Folklore Quarterly 18(1962): 3-12.

Studer views folklore and folk literature to be vital inclusions in a curriculum at a time when the world is more mobile than ever before. Folklore and literature offer several fine elements: an introduction to the creative arts; relates American heritage; aids in the development of regional roots; aids in the self concept of one's family or cultural roots; and serves as a bridge between peoples. "Folklore is not an escape into the age of homespun; it is an attempt to enrich today with the humanism of yesterday."

379.   Sussams, T. W.   "Fairy Stories and the Education of
Junior Pupils."   Journal of Education, March 1947, p. 124.

The author examines the attraction of fairy tales to
school children and is concerned when interest persists.
"This type of literature makes a universal appeal to
children under the age of six, but at about the normal
age of transfer from infant to junior schools boys
turn sharply against this kind of fantasy. Yet it is
not until the end of the junior school course that the
more intelligent girls tire of fairy stories and the
less gifted read them, surreptitiously perhaps, right
on into the middle years of adolescence." Tales bring
a catharsis to many of the deep-seated tensions of
childhood.

380.   Suzzallo, Henry.   "Introduction." In A Study of
Fairy Tales, by Laura Fry Kready. Boston: Houghton Mifflin,
1910.

To delete the fairy tale is to deny people their childhood, that transition period of much growth and understanding. Tales reflect the pulse and action of life
and must be shared with discrimination and skill for
it is only when well told that their educational riches
can be garnered.

381.   Tallman, Richard S.   "Folklore in the Schools: Teaching, Collecting and Publishing." New York Folklore Quarterly 28(1972): 163-186.

Tallman examines the uses and values of incorporating
folk literature into a school program. "The best way
to introduce students to folklore is to have them
collect it..." and often the greatest educational result in such cases is the students' learning to meet
and communicate with others. With folklore it is decidedly best to begin at home and have students read
and gather local folklore which is a part of their
everyday lives.

382.   Taylor, Pauline Byrd.   "Ethics in Fairy and Household Tales." Elementary English Review 17(1940): 190-191.

As folk tales are told solely for amusement, they have
no value in terms of teaching ethics. In fact, believes
Taylor, most are unethical and represent the thinking
of masses which is always below that of the individual.

383.   Taylor, Virginia.   "Storytelling: an Aside." Top of
the News, November 1967, pp. 8-10.

The author found story sharing to be a fine way of en-
couraging language growth when working with children
recently immigrated from Mexico. As the children shared
their folk tales in English their confidence grew as
did their English.

384. Towle, Carolyn. "The Value of Storytelling."
Grade Teacher, October 1947, p. 97.

Towle offers guidelines for the sharing of folk tales
and feels different types suit different times. Some
are for pure pleasure and others are for instruction.
Sad stories and scary ones should be omitted.

385. Towle, Carolyn. "What About Those Wrong Stories?"
American Childhood, January 1947, p. 12.

The author found it necessary to stress that fairy
tales were "pretend" stories before she shared them
so as to help the children in her class differentiate
between telling tales and telling lies.

386. Tucker, Nicholas. "Why Nursery Rhymes?" In Children
and Literature: Views and Reviews, edited by Virginia
Haviland. Glenview, Illinois: Scott, Foresman and Co.,
1973.

Tucker views nursery rhymes as ideally formed to aid
children in speech development. Language is explored
and stretched by way of rhymes as children use the
rhythm, alliteration and synonyms that fill them.
Nonsense rhymes show the child the sheer joy of words
as well as reinforcing logic. Through their references
to adult life, rhymes can introduce children to sexuality and death. In resonse to those concerned about
violence in rhymes, Tucker states that with "very few
exceptions, I find the violence in nursery rhymes to
be one of their major assets. They help to present
the child, at an early age, with a picture that makes
sense both of himself and of some of his feelings,
and also of aspects of the violent world around
him." At their simplest levels rhymes teach counting
and other skills. At their finest, rhymes can provide children a link with their inner selves. This
essay was originally published in Where, September
1969, pp. 152-155.

387 Turner, Klara. "Fairy Tales: a New Approach to
Reading Based on Predictability of Content and Language."
Reading, April 1978, pp. 29-35.

In working with children learning how to read, Turner
encourages the use of fairy tales both told and printed. Well known fairy tales provide children with a
reassurance and confidence when learning to read.
Children can tell their versions of fairy tales and
then read them in print as a method of beginning reading. Such tales and rhymes anchor the young child
to his culture.

388. Uspensky, Lev. "How Marvelous Are These Fairy Tales."
Anglo-Soviet Journal, May 1975, pp. 35-40.

Translated and reprinted from the Russian publication
Literaturnaya Gazeta (1974), the author defends the
artistry and riches of fairy tales for children. In
response to the standard negative viewpoints of tales
being useless or harmful to children, Uspensky points
out how very much of all the arts would have to be
censored if none of the fairy tales were allowed to
exist. All of the fairy tale characters and events
together "are our greatest helpers in educating future
generations of people who are, at once, both strong
and compassionate, vengeful and loving..."

389. van Stockum, Hilda. "Storytelling in the Family."
Horn Book 37(1961): 246-251.

The author recalls with fondness her childhood filled
with all variety of folk literature and storytelling.
In describing the values and influence storytelling
had on her development, van Stockum questions contemporary appeal of television and poorly made books.

390. Vaupel, Carol, and Others. "Using Folklore in Teaching Reading." ED 150 560. 1977.

Folklore offers three benefits as an aid to teaching
reading: (1)better understanding of society and self,
(2)relates to many other studies, and (3)gain better
and deeper insight into community. Vaupel shares
suggestions for the inclusion of folklore in the classroom.

391. Volc, Judy, and Stuart, Allaire. "Storytelling in
the Language Arts Program." Elementary English 45(1968):
958-965.

As a section of their language arts program the authors'
students learned and shared stories with their peers.
Children gained in regard to self confidence, story
plot awareness etc. and their amount of reading increased.

392. Walker, Louise Jean. "Moral Implications in Mother
Goose." Education, January 1960, pp. 292-293.

While nursery rhymes have overt values in terms of
learning skills such as counting, they also offer much
in regard to moral development. Good values can be
taught through the rhymes. "Mother Goose offers un-
limited opportunities for cultivating a real appreciation of what is good, noble, and inspiring without the
'goody-goody' element...From her lips, children effec-
tively learn emotional restraint, truth, and beauty."

393. Weber, Rosemary. "Traditional Materials for the
Youngest." Drexel Library Quarterly, October 1976,
pp. 32-41.

Mother Goose plays a significant role in every child's
cultural background. Books of rhymes help children
acquire numerous skills: facility with speech sounds
and patterns, arrangement of words and organization of
sounds and numbers. A bibliography is included.

394. Weiss, Gerhard H. "Folk Tale and Folklore: Useful
Tools For Teachers of German." ED 031 982. 1969.

Through the use of German folk tales students can learn
of the cultural differences between the United States
and Germany and differences within Germany as well.

395. Welsh, Charles. "Fairy Tales and the Trained Imagination." Dial, 16 May 1914, pp. 412-413.

In supporting the sharing of Grimm tales with children,
Welsh stresses their benefits toward the imagination.
Tales aid their development regarding command of rea-
son, control of will, and growth of moral sympathies.
Imagination is vital to man's growth and fairy tales
are vital as an aid toward imagination.

396. Wheelock, Lucy. "The Story." In Talks to Mothers.
Boston: Houghton Mifflin, 1920.

The author feels children are born with an interest
for story and that mothers who tell stories are the
first teachers of literature. As there is a tempta-
tion to pervert the story at school into something didactic or scientific, Wheelock sees the home as an
excellent place for the sharing of fairy tales with
children.

397. Wilcox, Leah. "The Artistry of Once Upon a Time."
Language Arts 52(1975): 983-986.

The classroom teacher who tells stories not only shares
enjoyment, but increases literary heritage, creative
powers, language and visualization. Empathy for
people of different areas and cultures can also be
gained by osmosis through these tales.

398. Wiltse, Sara. "The Purpose of the Story in the Kind-
dergarten." Journal of Proceedings and Addresses of the
35th Annual Meeting of the N.E.A. National Education
Association. 35(1896): 473-480.

The author heartily supports the use of story with
kindergarten children, but if a story does anything to
frighten a child it should not be shared. Tales of the

idle and tricky or of angelic children oppressed by
stepmothers representing all "feminine vices" should
not be used in the training of young children. For
the kindergartener Wiltse suggests Mother Goose, Lear
and other rhymes rather than "Little Red Riding Hood"
which so badly frightened her as a child.

399. Wittels, Fritz. "An Apology for Fairy Tales."
Child Study 9(1931): 67-69.

In examining fairy tales and children, Wittels views
tales as a valuable element in children's lives, but
that they should not be used as an integral part of
the curriculum. He is concerned too, that urban children cannot relate well to the world and mode of the
fairy tale. Yet, one must be very careful in the rewriting or updating of fairy tales for it is an impossible task and should not be done. "The fairy tale
in its lovely innocence is in harmony with the mind
of the child, compromising the wishes of the child with
the demands of ethics.

400. Wycke, Richard T. "Storytelling." Education,
October 1907, pp. 76-79.

The author found that a classics curriculum could be
centered around storytelling. Grammar was directly
related to storytelling as well as art, drama, spelling,
geography etc. Beyond all else, through storytelling
fine literature was being shared.

401. Yolen, Jane. "How Basic is SHAZAM?" Language Arts
54(1977): 645-651.

Yolen urges the re-introduction of classical mythology
to contemporary children brought up on the shallow
myths of television. When myth is removed from a
child's life language and art are damaged. Mythology
also leads children to an understanding of themselves.

402. Young, Sue Morgan. A Study of Contemporary Views
Concerning the Use of Fairy Tales in the Fourth, Fifth,
and Sixth Grades. Master's thesis, Tennessee Polytechnic
Institute, 1961.

Young examined the use of fairy tales in readers for
upper elementary students. Criteria for tales included were explored and suggestions are made for
methods of using fairy tales and related activities.
Areas of study discussed in regard to fairy tales include science, language arts, social studies and basic
skills of reading, writing and arithmetic. Young concludes by recommending that more tales be included in
elementary readers, however, "the teacher should know
each child and his need before teaching any fairy
tale to the class."

403. Young, Tommie, ed. "The Child's Literary Heritage:
Folk and Fairy Literature." ED 069 299. 1972.

Young reports on a workshop on folk literature and
children held at North Carolina Central University
in July 1972. Time was spent working with adults to
understand the humanizing and much needed effect of
tales upon children. Suggestions for stories and their
selection are included, as well as techniques for telling stories when working with different age groups.

404. Zehm, Stanley. "Promoting Language Growth Through
Nursery Rhymes." _Elementary English_ 52(1975): 141-142.

As a manner of extending writing and vocabulary skills,
Zehm had his upper elementary students rewrite standard nursery rhymes in elaborate "Thesaurus" style.
The children enjoyed the project and began such rewriting of complete stories.

PSYCHOLOGY

405. Abrams, Joan. "How Content and Symbolism in Mother
Goose May Contribute to the Development of a Child's Integrated Psyche." ED 153 220. 1977.

Abrams analyzes Mother Goose rhymes in relation to the
psychological stages of child development. These
stages are then discussed in terms of the child's basic
needs as defined by Bettelheim in The Uses of Enchantment. Contents of rhymes are viewed in regard to
human nature, needs and sexuality.

406. Alexander, Lloyd. "Identifications and Identities."
Wilson Library Bulletin 45(1970): 144-148.

Born with no true identity, Alexander feels we grow from
childhood through folk tales to which we respond emo-
tionally rather than by intellect. As children develop their own identities via tales these same tales
establish our bond with all peoples and all times.

407. "Are Fairy Tales Outgrown?" Literary Digest, 29
November 1919, p. 32.

The child is far from a fragile being that must be
protected from fairy tales. To deny fairy tales is to
deny children full emotional preparation for adulthood.

408. "Are Gory Fairy Tales an Evil?" Literary Digest,
5 January 1929, pp. 20-21.

Quoting from Die Umschau by two psychologists, this
article stresses the overall values of children's
exposure to tales and the subconscious connection
between tales and our ancestral memories. While adult
difficulties can often be traced to childhood, it is
rare that the dreadful events related in fairy tales
and folk tales have such an influence. "It is important for the tale to be told by one intelligent and
sympathetic in nature." The tales provide for all who
listen a form of psychological release.

409. Bailey, Carolyn Sherwin. "Imagination and the Fairy
Story." In For the Story Teller. Springfield, Mass.:
Milton Bradley, 1916.

Fairy tales aid greatly in the growth of a child's imagination, but these tales must be carefully selected.
Tales such as "Blue Beard" or "Ali Baba" do little but
cause children nightmares and give them ideas of
cruelty, vengence and crime.

410. Bettelheim, Bruno. "Bringing Up Children: In Praise
of Fairy Tales." Ladies Home Journal, October 1973,
pp. 32-33 and November 1973, pp. 38-39.

A brief article explores Bettelheim's views and analysis of fairy tales and their importance to children's
lives. Tales examined here are "The Three Little Pigs"
and "The Ant and the Grasshopper." The second half of
this two part article discusses the tales "Hansel and
Gretel" and "Little Red Riding Hood."

411. Bettleheim, Bruno. "The Importance of Fairy Tales."
Instructor, August 1976, pp. 79-80.

An adapted excerpt from the author's book The Uses of
Enchantment: the Meaning and Importance of Fairy Tales.

412. Bettelheim, Bruno. "Reflections." New Yorker,
8 December 1975, pp. 50-114.

Bettelheim's initial publication of his core ideas
later printed in The Uses of Enchantment. Here the
author analyzes several tales, compares them to contemporary literature and discusses the richness of
orally sharing fairy tales with children.

413. Briehl, Marie. "A Psychoanalytic Point of View on
the Use of Fairy Tales in the Education of Young Children."
Reiss-Davis Clinic Bulletin, Spring 1976, pp. 28-44.

414. Brown, Marcia. "The Hero Within." Elementary
English 44(1967): 201-207.

In speaking of her own work and the role of literature
(including folk literature) in a child's interior development, Brown disucsses the rich spirit and support
tales offer children. Tales may aid children in their
search for Self. Tales allow children the total risk
of one's self. They can provide the "key that will un-
lock life to them, will reveal the hero within."

415. Buhler, Karl. "Fairy Tales and Their Relation to the
Child." In The Mental Development of the Child. New
York: Harcourt Brace and Co., 1930.

Buhler discusses the various age interests in fairy
tales and psychological analysis. The fairy tale con-
tains rapid and varied changes of image content, sim-
ultaneous combinations of ideas, methods of exaggera-
tion and avoids all thinking which is at all compli-
cated. Buhler states "poetic allusions, metaphors
etc. are completely abscent in fairy tales."

416.   Cath, Stanley, and Cath, Claire. "On the Other Side
of OZ: Psychoanalytic Aspects of Fairy Tales." Psychoanalytic Study of the Child 33(1978): 621-639.

Though the authors analyze The Wizard of Oz, their
hypothesis and conclusions are addressed to fairy tales
as well. As dreams, favorite fairy tales screen un-
resolved psychic issues to which the child must return
until a point of resolution. The intensity of this
experience leads many children to select only particular adults with whom to share the experience. The
way a tale is read or told also affects this process.

417.   Chesterton, G. K. "The Ethics of Elfland." In
Orthodoxy. New York: Dodd, 1909.

Chesterton writes of his values and beliefs that have
their core in his childhood. "The things I believed
most then, the things I believe most now, are the
things called fairy tales...I am concerned with a certain way of looking at life, which was created in me
by the fairy tales, but has since been meekly rati-
fied by the mere facts." The author sees belief in
fairy tales as quite different from sentimentality.

418.   Chesterton, G. K. "The Red Angel." In Tremendous
Trifles. New York: Sheed and Ward, 1955.

Believing that "the fear does not come from fairy tales;
the fear comes from the universe of the soul," the
author supports children's exposure to folk tales. Tales
accustom children to the unknown elements ahead and offer
them the first clear idea of the possible defeat of
the fearful and alarming.

419.   Datan, Nancy. "Narcissism of the Life Cycle: the
Dialectics of Fairy Tales." Human Development 20(1977):
191-199.

Acknowledging Bettelheim's theories, Datan goes on to
discuss the values of fairy tales in regard to presenting the complexities and various behaviors of adulthood to the individual's childhood. Focusing on
"Hansel and Gretel," "Snow White," and "The Emperor's
New Clothes," Datan explores the literary presentation
of adults with finite resources, latent fears and the
capacity for evil.

420. de Carvalho-Neto, Paulo. "Metapsychology." In
Folklore and Psychoanalysis, translated by Jacques Wilson.
Coral Gables, Floriaa: University of Miami Press, 1972.

The author disucsses children's sexuality and related
developments using Freud's theories. Folk literature
is filled with symbolism just as are dreams and relate
to children and their unconscious needs and desires.

421. "Defending Fairy Tales." Literary Digest, 21 November
1931, p. 19.

This brief article quotes a review of Apology for Fairy
Tales (circa 1931) which worked to calm apprehensive
parents and assure them that the "innocence" of fairy
tales was in keeping with childhood.

422. Dieckmann, Hans. "The Favourite Fairy Tale of Childhood." Journal of Analytical Psychology, January 1971,
pp. 18-30.

Dieckmann discusses the use of a patient's favorite
childhood fairy tale as a part of analysis. As fairy
tales are most frequent during the same period of childhood as that time in which fundamental neurotic patterns
are laid down connections are likely. As fairy tales
are "among the earliest cultural products absorbed by
the human soul" they can be used as a diagnostic tool
in determining neurotic archetypal fixations.

423. Dundes, Alan and Others. "Strategy of Turkish Boy's
Verbal Duelling Rhymes." Journal of American Folklore
83(1970): 325-349.

The authors examine the Turkish folk-word game of one
ups-manship that is similar to playing the dozens in
the United States. The contesting is based on sexuality and the winner's dominance of the loser who is
seen in a passive homosexual role. "The duel affords
the young Turkish boy an opportunity to give appropriate vent to the emotional concomitants of the pain-
ful process of becoming a man."

424. Ehrlich, Phyllis. "Once Again: Once Upon a Time."
New York Times Magazine, 25 December 1960, p. 19.

Storytelling and folk tales told by parents to child-
dren help to increase parent-child rapport, a sense of
continuity and can lead to an awareness of their own
family past.

425. "Fairy Tales Told Children Blamed for Later Ills."
Science Newsletter, 6 March 1937, p. 153.

A report of the 1937 meeting of the American Orthro-
psychiatric Association at which Sandor Lorand stated
that many of the mental and emotional troubles of
adults can be traced to the fairy tales they heard
during childhood. Lorand also stated that the way a
tale is told is as important as the tale itself.

426. Freud, Sigmund. "The Occurance in Dreams of Material
From Fairy-Tales." In On Creativity and the Unconscious:
Papers on the Psychology of Art, Literature, Love, Reli-
gion, selected by Benjamin Nelson. New York: Harper and
Brothers, 1958.

Elements of fairy tales are fequently found in dreams
and Freud discusses two cases where therapy evolved
from the patient's memories of "Little Red Riding Hood"
and "The Wolf and the Seven Little Kids." For many,
a recollection of favorite fairy tales replaces memories of their own childhood. Freud felt it not surprising "that psycho-analysis confirms us in our recognition of how great an influence folk fairy-tales have
upon the mental life of our children."

427. Gardner, Howard. "Brief on Behalf of Fairy."
Phaedrus 5(1978): 14-23.

Gardner discusses with praise Bettelheim's The Uses of
Enchantment. Balanced with the acclaim are thoughtful
questions regarding Bettelheim's view of childhood.
Much of the Bettelheim book can be accepted only if
one accepts his Freudian views. Gardner sees the book
as a brief that "proceeds beyond the evidence" to per-
suade, and urges much further study of the interaction
of fairy tales and children. Also questioned are the
book's applications to non-European cultures and folk
literature.

428. Garthwaite, Marion. "The Acid Test." Horn Book
39(1963): 408-411.

Witches and other wicked characters in folk tales are
like lemons. They must be tart and zestful in order to
do what they need to do in a story. Watered down orgres
leave a tale limp and disappointing. Children may
cringe and gasp during fearful tales, but they want to.
They need to, and welcome the harshness of fairy tale
judgements.

429. Gentry, W. Doyle. "Agression in Fairy Tales: Com-
parison of Three Cultures." Psychological Reports
37(1975): 895-898.

Based on the theory that children learn behaviors
through vicarious learning as well as experiential,
Gentry analyzed fairy tales from Japan, middle-eastern
India and the Grimm collection. While all cultures'

tales contained agression, the Grimm tales most popular in the United States depicted significantly more
human agression than those tales of the other two
cultures.

430.   Goldings, Herbert J.   "Jump-Rope Rhymes and the
Rhythm of Latency Development in Girls." In The Psycho-
analytic Study of the Child. Vol. 29.   New Haven: Yale
University Press, 1974.

Goldings examines the variety, role and analysis of
jump-rope rhymes used by girls during ages six to
eleven.   Jumping rope is seen as a highly sensual
experience that, while disguised and ritualized, is
filled with images of sexual activity.

431.   Green, George H.   Psychanalysis in the Classroom.
New York: Putnam, 1922.   pp. 65-78 and 214-218.

For the child the fairy tale is a reflection of his
own life.   It is a world where he is often surrounded
by greater powers and filled with intense antitheses.
Such a world matches his own where justice is quick
and severe.   The fairy tale is also attractive to the
child for it takes him beyond the struggling present
and into a resolved future of "Happy every afters."
Green discusses "Cinderella" as an example of such
child identification.   "The fairy tale that appeals to
the child makes its appeal because it is all about
himself."

432.   Gruenberg, Sidonie Matsner.   We, the Parents: Our
Relationship to Our Children and to the World Today.
New York: Harper and Brothers, 1939.   pp. 192-196.

Gruenberg responds to challenges made against fairy
tales and views them as the mode of expression that is
especially congenial to the child.   A child who becomes
fixated with a tale has problems beyond the fairy tale
and the tale cannot be blamed.   If children can vent
frustrations by reading, hearing or acting out "Jack
and the Giant Killer," Gruenberg feels they will be
all the better for the experience.

433.   Hartmann, Waltraut.   "Identification and Projection
in Folk Fairy-Tales and in Fantastic Stories for Children."
Bookbird 7(1969): 8-17.

Hartmann explores the psychological relationship of
children to folk literature on various levels.   Children quickly identify with fairy tale heroes and imi-
tate their attitudes.   Such identification is closely
linked to a child's understanding the meaning of the
story.   As the child grows he is able to understand
increasingly complex hero figures.   Related to this
is the child's adoption of literary heroes as projection figures.

434. Haughton, Rosemary. "Introduction." In Tales From
Eternity: The World of Fairy Tales and the Spiritual
Search. New York: Seabury Press, 1973.

As basically symbolic and of the past, fairy tales
provide a link to the Christian past and its pagan
prehistory. "Fairy-tales can open our minds to the
human, and make us able to hear more sharply the de-
mand for the transformation of the human into its own
completeness in Christ."

435. Heisig, James W. "Bruno Bettelheim and the Fairy
Tales." Children's Literature. Vol. 6. Annual of the
Modern Language Association Group on Children's Literature
and The Children's Literature Association. Philadelphia:
Temple University Press, 1977.

Heisig offers a criticism welcoming Bettelheim's research in The Uses of Enchantment. Points challenged
include the sexuality of fairy tales and the child's
domination of tales.

436. Heuscher, Julius E. "Folklore, Westerns and Crime
Stories: With Comments on the Effect of Television." In
A Psychiatric Study of Myths and Fairy Tales: Their Origin,
Meaning and Usefulness. Springfield, Illinois: Charles
Thomas Publisher, 1974.

Addressing the question of ill effects from fairy tales
as opposed to television, Heuscher notes that while
television play among children is actualistic and un-
controlled the playing out of folk literature is play-
ful and filled with joy. While any tale could cause
fear in a given child, the manner and times at which
tales are shared have much to do with such effects.

437. Heuscher, Julius E. "Human Development." In A Psy-
chiatric Study of Myths and Fairy Tales: Their Origin,
Meaning and Usefulness. Springfield, Illinois: Charles
Thomas Publisher, 1974.

Heuscher investigates the three primary stages of child
development. Fairy tales which deal with children also
fall into these areas: (a)early childhood, (b)latency
period and (c)adolescence. While sharing cultural and
ethical aspects, fairy tales illuminate these various
periods of development. Tales discussed in relation
to development include: (a)"Hansel and Gretel" and
"Little Red Riding Hood," (b)"Snow White," "The Wolf
and the Seven Little Kids," and "The Juniper Tree"
and (c)"Sleeping Beauty," "Treadeschin," and "The
Dragon in the Black Woods."

438. Hillman, James. "A Note on Story." <u>Parabola</u>
4(1979): 43-45.

Hillman sees tales and story not as something to be
taught or studied, but as a way of living--"a way in
which the soul finds itself in life." A childhood
built with stories allows one a better relation to
dream and fantasy as an adult. Hillman stresses a
Jungian approach to story and finds traditional tales
the richest and the best. "The main body of Biblical
and classical tales direct fantasy into organized,
deeply life-giving psychological patterns, these
stories present the archetypal modes of experiencing."
This essay was also printed in <u>Children's Literature</u>
3(1974): 9-11.

439. Hafer, Marie Rose. <u>A Study of the Favorite Childhood</u>
<u>Fairy Tales of An Adult Psychiatric Population</u>. Doctoral
dissertation, California School of Professional Psychology,
1976.

Adult patients were questioned about their favorite
fairy tale from childhood. By using a Jungian conception of archetypes, observations showed that one's per-
sonalized version of a tale proved significant as a
diagnostic Gestalt and reflected the overall psychic
make up of the individual. The identification with the
entire tale supported theories of the impact of classic
fairy tales on the development of the psyche.

440. Hohman, Leslie B. "As the Twig is Bent: Daydreams
and Fairy Tales Have Their Uses." <u>Ladies Home Journal</u>,
April 1940, pp. 147-148.

Hohman, a doctor of psychiatry, believes children
should be exposed to fairy tales and nursery rhymes,
but that one should never let them forget that they
are "only pleasant foolery."

441. Johnson, N. M. "Shelter Stories." <u>Junior Bookshelf</u>,
July 1942, pp. 45-48.

Johnson discusses her use of folk literature in story
hours held in airraid shelters in England during World
War II. Folk tales were espcially appropriate for
they were known to the children and served as suppor-
tive friends while their immediate world was filled
with darkness, raids, and the noise of bombs. In telling tales such as "Cinderella" and "Hansel and Gretel,"
the author was hoping to fill the children's dreams
with thoughts more pleasant than the war.

442. Le Gallienne, Richard. "Concerning Fairy Tales." In
<u>Attitudes and Avowals: With Some Retrospective Reviews</u>.
New York: John Lane Co., 1910.

Defining the fairy tale as a heavenly story with an
earthly meaning, the author finds the tales most accepted by all ages to be those that recognize the human
need of supernatural aid and alleviation. A list of
the twelve "best" fairy tales is included.

443. Le Guin, Ursula. "The Child and the Shadow." In
The Language of the Night: Essays on Fantasy and Science
Fiction, edited by Susan Wood. New York: Putnam, 1979.

Using Andersen's tale "The Man Without a Shadow" and
Jungian theories, Le Guin explores the qualities of
folk literature and fantasy that deal with the evil/
shadow elements of everyone. By sharing such tales
with children Le Guin believes children are more able
to face their own shadows, learn to control them and
be positively guided by them as opposed to being ruled
by one's fears. This essay was first printed in
Quarterly Journal of the Library of Congress, April,
1975.

444. L'Engle, Madeleine. "What is Real?" Language Arts
55(1978): 447-451.

In this age of pollution and mechanization, L'Engle
feels fairy tales are as important as ever. By sharing
such tales with children we enter the real world, the
world of the whole person and all have a greater chance
of becoming whole and free.

445. Lorand, Sandor. "Fairy Tales and Neurosis."
The Psychoanalytic Quarterly 4(1935): 234-243.

While it is difficult to form any definite opinion regarding fairy tales and their possible harmful effects,
their positive attributes must be recognized. While
some illness may be related to fairy tales, fairy tales
do not in themselves cause the neurosis. A tale that
gave comfort as a child may become a core of anxieties
as an adult. Caution and consideration in telling
tales is paramount.

446. Lorand, Sandor. "Fairy Tales, Lilliputian Dreams
and Neurosis." The American Journal of Orthopsychiatry
7(1937): 456-464.

Through case examples, Lorand discusses the role of the
fairy tale to neurotic dreams and behavior, most especially dreams of the Lilliputian genre. Lorand believes
the content and manner of telling tales to children
may leave enduring impressions and could add to causes
of neurotic illness.

447.   Melani, Lilia.   "A Child's Psyche: Recollections of
Fairy Tales, Myths and Romances."   The Lion and the Unicorn
3(1979): 14-27.

The author writes of her intensely personal involvement
with folk literature as a child.   Both in retrospect
and at the time, she found strength and support in
many of the tales she read while being frightened by
others--especially Andersen.   Melani grew from her
reading of tales and feels "There is a tale for every
child which if found, will enlarge the child's world
and experience of self, quiet fears, provide comfort
and send the child toward adulthood...with a newly
acquired reserve of strength."

448.   Partridge, Emelyn, and Partridge, George.   "The Story-
Telling Situation."   In Storytelling in School and Home.
New York: Sturgis and Walton, 1912.

Partridge addresses the complex relationship between
teller and story listener.   As in all art, the experience shared affects all elements of those involved.
As the teller tells the tale he is educating deep desires within the child and the child is evaluating
and selecting,out of which will come the ideals and
character that will define his life.

449.   Quigley, May G.   "Telling Stories."   Public Libraries
10(1905): 351-353.

Quigley feels storytelling has greatly benefited from
psychology and that the best tales to tell are fairy
tales.   It is the spiritual life of the fairy people
more than themselves that attract children "for it
is this life which furnishes them something by which
they can measure the same life within themselves."
The author feels moralizing should be avoided, and
sarcasm and irony should be left out of stories for
young audiences.

450.   Ricklin, Franz.   "Wishfulfillment and Symbolism in
Fairy Tales."   Nervous and Mental Disease Monograph Series.
No. 21.   Translated by Dr. William A. White.   New York:
Nervouse and Mental Disease Publishing Co., 1915.

Ricklin examines the elements of wish structure and
symbolism in fairy tales.   A wide variety of European
tales are analized and compared in regard to their
symbolism they share with dreams.   Ricklin, as did
Freud, feels the psychology of the fairy tale "stands
in close relationship to the world of dreams, of hys-
teria, and of mental disease...It is surprising how
great a role the sexual plays in fairy tales and how
great is the agreement of the sexual symbolism with
that of dreams and psychopathology...although the fairy

tales appear to us in a new, less childlike garb. They
lose, on that account, nothing of their charm and power
of attraction."

451. Ross, Ramon. "Folk Tales For Young Children."
ED 022 620. 1968.

Folk tales far out shine literature written for basal
readers. Folk literature allows the child the chance
to look inside himself. While contemporary stories
deal with children in general, fairy tales deal with
the Self. With fairy tales, the child can vicariously
experience that which is to come.

452. Rubenstein, Ben. "The Meaning of the Cinderella
Story in the Development of a Little Girl." American
Imago 12(1955): 197-205.

The author offers a Freudian interpretation of his
young daughters attachment to "Cinderella" and her
sexual frustrations. He concludes "that the identification with the fairy tale...was already a portent
of the coming latency or the long waiting sleep like
that of Sleeping Beauty. Expressed in the identification was the tacit recognition of her minute clitoris
with accompanying phantasies of castration and being
beaten masochistically by the father."

453. Scherf, Walter. "Family Conflicts and Emancipation
in Fairy Tales." Children's Literature 3(1975): 77-93.

After investigating numerous tales, Scherf believes
that children's so-called magic tales reflect basic
family conflicts and which push the child forward to
emancipation. These tales exist to help listeners
reach ideal adulthood. Tales of Perrault and the
Grimm brothers are discussed.

454. Shea, John. "Theology and Autobiography."
Commonweal, 16 June 1978, pp. 358-362.

Shea discusses the values and richness of story in all
lives and especially as a way of emotional healing
and growth. Stories that reach the child or adult are
then able to stretch him into new areas of thought
and view.

455. Sonkin, Janice. "Folklore in an English Infant
School." In "Early Childhood Socialization in Great Britian:
Bradford Field Study Program," edited by Marijean Suelzle
and Others. ED 156 991. 1977.

Sonkin's research and collecting of children's folk
literature came to show that children use their lore
and rhymes and riddles and tales to (1)gain prestige
and (2)cope with present situations. Children develop
a teacher-child language and a child to child language,
the latter of which is the language of their folk
literature.

456. Spock, Benjamin. "Are Fairy Tales Good for Children."
Redbook, June 1976, pp. 22-23.

Spock urges parents not to become too upset over the
various views concerning fairy tales and children.
He believes a primary factor in this question should
be the age of the child.

457. Walker, Louise Jean. "Humor in Mother Goose."
Progressive Education, March 1954, pp. 150-151.

The author discusses the humor in most Mother Goose
rhymes and cites several examples of word plays and
absurd events. It is the fun of the rhymes that keeps
them alive. "Our psychologists tell us that the kind
of thing one laughs at is a dependable indication of
one's mental and emotional balance. A child's laughter
is hearty and gay, and the wholesome fun in Mother Goose
rhymes and nonsense poetry is calculated to keep it
so.

458. Walker, Virginia, and Lunz, Mary E. "Symbols, Fairy
Tales and School-Age Children." Elementary School Journal,
November 1976, pp. 94-100.

Basing their study on theories of Jung and von Franz,
the authors had children draw a picture after hearing
a telling of "Snow White and Rose Red." Results supported the hypothesis that tales told orally encourage
children to experience the symbols of the tales--sym-
bols that are passed through time and bind all human
beings together. Their pictures represented not specific scenes, but rather the children's impressions of
the entire story. The authors also discuss symbolism
and the connection between present telling and the
past.

459. Wheeler, H. E. "Psychological Case Against the Fairy
Tale." Elementary School Journal, June 1929, pp. 754-755.

Quoting two psychologists (Dr. Harry Overstreet and Dr.
Alfred Adler), Wheeler points out the dangers of telling
fairy tales to children. Tales are felt to pervert the
imaginative life and they should be drastically ruled
out of a child's life as are terrorizing nurse maids
and hell-preaching religionists. Stories that include
ghosts, goblins, miraculous achievements and non-
scientific explanations of natural phenomena should be
kept from children.

460.   Winkler, Franz.   "Information and Education." In
Man, the Bridge Between Two Worlds.   New York: Harper
and Row, 1960.

Winkler urges one to remember that when a tale is told
to a child it is dealing with man's soul--his inner
life.   Those who try to protect children by rewriting
tales are overly sentimental for "many years of caring
for problem children have convinced us of the protection from anxiety and criminal urges that folklore
affords."   When respected, the fairy tale serves as a
child's natural guide to religion.

461.   Wolfenstein, Martha.   "Children's Books: Parents,
Children and Fairy Tales."   Child Study 24(1947): 56-57.

The author dismantles negative criticism of fairy tales
such as violence, stepmother, and as being non-realis-
tic, and discusses the way different aged children
respond to tales.   Fairy tales are not for every child
and should not be forced on one who dislikes them.

462.   Wolkstein, Diane.   "Old and New Sexual Messages in
Fairy Tales."   Wilson Library Bulletin 46(1971): 162-166.

Wolkstein discusses the sensual and sexual messages
inherent in tales that children and adults request
time and again.   Fairy tales do not deal directly with
the moment of intercourse.   Instead, "what is portrayed
by some of the old fairy tales is the atmosphere and
feelings of the female and male prior to and after the
state of consummation."   "Cinderella," "The Twelve
Dancing Princesses," and "Sleeping Beauty" are examined
in regard to their sensuality and sexuality.   Tales
stress patience, persistance and courage, all that
apply to sexual enjoyment.

463.   Wood, Grace.   "What Lies Behind Fairy Tales."
Contemporary Review, June 1954, pp. 364-367.

Wood views traditional fairy tales as adult tales that
are imitations of the spiritual world.   She explains
the child's fascination with such a tale because "in
it he sees his own situations, Mother Kind, Mother
Cross, Father Loving, Father Big and Angry, and sees
himself by enchantment as conqueror."   "Sleeping
Beauty" and "Little Red Riding Hood" are discussed.

464.   Zipes, Jack.   "On the Use and Abuse of Folk and Fairy
Tales With Children: Bruno Bettelheim's Moralistic Magic
Wand."   In Breaking the Magic Spell: Radical Theories of
Folk and Fairy Tales.   Austin: University of Texas Press,
1979.

Zipes challenges Bettelheim's theories on children and fairy tales on psychological and literary grounds. Believing Bettelheim to have misrepresented Freudian psychology, Zipes offers his own analysis of "Cinderella" and other motifs. As literature, Zipes feels Bettelheim misrepresents their symbolism by failing to look beyond the middle ages.

465.   Zumwalt, Rosemary.   "Plain and Fancy: a Content Analysis of Children's Jokes Dealing With Adult Sexuality." Western Folklore 35(1976): 258-267.

Children have their own sexual folk literature filled with parents failing to answer questions truthfully and jokes regarding intercourse. Because the child sees his body as being so unlike his parent's he has no immediate connection between sexuality and himself.

AUTHOR INDEX

A

Abrams, Joan   405
Adler, Felix   195, 196
Aitken, Johan L.   197
Alexander, Lloyd   406
Allen, Arthur   198
Alvey, Richard Gerald   1
Anderson, William   199, 200
Applebee, Arthur   2
Arbuthnot, May Hill   3
Aries, Philippe   4
Arlitt, Ada Hart   5
Armstrong, Helen   6
Auden, W. H.   8, 9

B

Babcock, Mildred D.   10
Bailey, Carolyn Sherwin
   201, 202, 203, 204, 205,
   409
Bailey, W. L.   206
Baker, Christine H.   11
Barbara A. Kilpatrick,
   Sister   125
Bard, Therese Jeanne Bissen
   207
Baruch, Dorothy   208
Batalla, Benjamin C.   209
Baudouin, Charles   210
Bauman, Richard   211
Beard, Patten   212
Beck, Josephine Bristal
   213
Becker, May Lamberton   12
Bettelheim, Bruno   410, 411,
   412
Betzner, Jean   13
Bingham, Jane   214
Bino, Marial   215
Blos, Joan   216
Bodger, Andrew   217
Bodger, Joan   14
Bonner, Mary Graham   15
Bowen, Elizabeth   16

Boyd, Gertrude   218
Bradley, J. B.   219
Brady, Margaret Katheryne
   17
Brewster, Paul   220
Briehl, Marie   413
Briggs, Nancy E.   221
Brooks, Jeanne R.   18
Brose, Patricia Bernice
   Dunn   222
Brown, Gilbert L.   223
Brown, Marcia   414
Bruce, H.   19
Brun, Victor   20
Bryant, Margaret M.   224
Bryant, Sara Cone   225, 226
Buchan, Vivian   227
Buhler, Karl   415
Butler, Helen L.   228
Byers, Nell B.   229

C

Callaway, Lynn   21
Capek, Karel   22
Carlson, Ruth Kearney   230
Carr, John C.   313
Castle, E. B.   231
Cath, Claire   416
Cath, Stanley   416
Cather, Katherine D.   232
Cawthorne, Edythe   23
Chambers, Dewey W.   233, 234
Chaparro, Jacqueline L.
   235
Chesterton, G. K.   24, 25,
   417, 418
Chubb, Percival   236
Chukovsky, Kornei   237
Clark, Carol   26
Cober, Mary E.   238
Coggins, Herbert L.   27
Coleman, Mrs. Thomas   239
Colgan, Richard T.   240

TITLE INDEX

T

SUBJECT INDEX

About the Compiler

GEORGE W. B. SHANNON is a freelance writer and storyteller. His previous works include *Humpty Dumpty: A Pictorial History*, *Lizard's Song*, and *The Gang and Mrs. Higgins*.